Preschool Programming of
Children With Disabilities

(Second Printing)

Preschool Programming of Children With Disabilities

Edited by

ROGER REGER

Director of Special Education Programs
Board of Cooperative Educational Services
Erie County (Buffalo), New York

CHARLES C THOMAS · PUBLISHER
Springfield • Illinois • U.S.A.

Published and Distributed Throughout the World by

CHARLES C THOMAS   PUBLISHER

Bannerstone House

301-327 East Lawrence Avenue, Springfield, Illinois, U.S.A.

1970, by CHARLES C THOMAS   PUBLISHER

ISBN 0-398-01564-3

Library of Congress Catalog Card Number: 70-103584

First Printing, 1970
Second Printing, 1974

*With THOMAS BOOKS careful attention is given to all details of
manufacturing and design. It is the Publisher's desire to present books that are
satisfactory as to their physical qualities and artistic possibilities and
appropriate for their particular use. THOMAS BOOKS will be true to those
laws of quality that assure a good name and good will.*

Printed in the United States of America
R-1

CONTRIBUTORS

MRS. JEANETTE BURKE received her B.S. degree in 1961 from the State University College of Education at Buffalo in the field of orthopedic handicap. She was part of the team that worked on the Standardized Perkins-Binet Intelligence Test which should be published in the early 1970's. She has worked as a teacher-consultant in the program for students with visual disabilities for the Board of Cooperative Educational Services of Erie County (Buffalo), New York.

MRS. NANCY L. DETRICK received her B.S. degree in 1967 from Murray State University with majors in elementary education and English. She works with young children with serious learning problems for the Board of Cooperative Educational Services.

MRS. MARIAN KOPPMANN received her B.S. degree in 1965 from the University College of New York at Buffalo and her M.S. degree in 1969 from the same institution. Her major field has been special education. She has taught special classes of young children with serious learning problems and most recently has been in charge of a Child Evaluation Center in the Board of Cooperative Educational Services.

MRS. LOIS MOULIN received her B.A. degree in 1967 in the field of home economics education from the State University College at Buffalo, having spent a brief period of time at the Merrill-Palmer Institute in Detroit. She has worked with young children who have serious learning problems and she was a teacher in the summer program described in her chapter. She also has worked with preschool children in the Child Evaluation Center in the Board of Cooperative Educational Services.

MISS SANDRA H. PERLEY received her B.S. degree in 1965 in special education from the State University College at Buffalo and currently is completing work on a master's degree. She was a teacher in the summer preschool program described in her chapter. She has taught special classes of young mentally retarded children, worked as an itinerant teacher-consultant of children with visual disabilities, and as a teacher in the Child Evaluation Center in the Board of Cooperative Educational Services. Most recently she accepted a temporary position as Coordinator of Programs for the Handicapped during a vacancy created by a sabbatical leave.

ROGER REGER received his B.A. degree in psychology from the University of Texas in 1957, his M.A. degree in psychology from the same institution in 1958, his M.A. Ed. degree in educational administration and special education from Eastern Michigan University (Ypsilanti) in 1962, and was enrolled in a doctoral program in special education at the University of Michigan. He has been director of special education programs since 1965 for the Board of Cooperative Educational Services. His two other books are SCHOOL PSYCHOLOGY, published in 1965 by Charles C Thomas, Publisher, and SPECIAL EDUCATION: CHILDREN WITH LEARNING PROBLEMS, coauthored by Wendy Schroeder and Kathy Uschold, published in 1968 by Oxford University Press.

MRS. BETH CHAPMAN RINGQUIST received her B.S. degree in 1968 from the State University College at Fredonia (New York) in the field of speech pathology and audiology. In 1969 she received her M.S. degree in the same field from the Fredonia institution.

MISS SUSANNE ROBERTS received her B.S. Ed. degree in 1965 in the field of special education from the State University College of New York at Buffalo, and her M.S. Ed. from the same college in 1969. She has worked as a teacher of young mentally retarded children with a special interest in materials for young children.

TIMOTHY ROCHFORD received his B.S. degree in 1965 in special education from the State University College of New York at Buffalo, and his M.S. in the same field from the Buffalo college in 1966. He joined the staff of the Board of Cooperative Educational Services as a teacher of young children with serious learning problems and since then has been an assistant supervisor for the program. He is enrolled in a doctoral program at the State University of New York at Buffalo.

MRS. WENDY SCHROEDER received her B.A. degree in 1961 in elementary education and speech and hearing from the State University College of New York at Buffalo, and her M.A. degree in speech pathology in 1966 from the State University of New York at Buffalo. She is coauthor with Reger and Uschold of SPECIAL EDUCATION: CHILDREN WITH LEARNING PROBLEMS, published in 1968 by Oxford University Press. She has worked as a speech correctionist, as a classroom teacher of young children with serious learning problems, and as a supervisor of the program for the Board of Cooperative Educational Services.

MRS. JOAN KRAUSS TEACH received her B.A. degree in 1960 in elementary education from Wittenberg University and her M.S. degree in 1965 in special education from Purdue University. She was a Perceptual Motor Therapist at N. C. Kephart's Achievement Center for Children at Purdue University from 1963 to 1966. She also was director of the Motor Laboratory Program at the Achievement Center and an instructor in the graduate program. She works as a special consultant for the Board of Cooperative Educational Services.

MRS. MARY LANG and MRS. JOAN COBB are parents of children with learning problems and members of the Western New York Association for Children with Learning Disabilities.

PREFACE

My first contact with preschool children with disabilities was at a temporary "home" for delinquent and neglected children associated with the juvenile court in Travis County, Austin, Texas. At that time the very young children were considered disabled only because they were neglected by their parents, which almost always meant their mothers, as fathers typically were absent. I recall vividly one instance where a five-year-old black child and his two younger siblings were brought to the home. The five-year-old, it was discovered, was attending school but before leaving each morning he prepared breakfast for himself and his siblings, and upon returning from school he took care of lunch and other routine household chores. In his absence his next-younger sibling took charge. My colleagues and I were all white, middle-class types, either university students or recent-students temporarily undecided about what we really wanted to do.

We had a difficult time understanding the speech of the five-year-old, as well as the other two. One statement finally translated by the young lady in charge of the group still stays with me, and it sounded something like this: "I' se y' chokiepie?" We interpreted the statement to be a "playful" question: "Am I your sugar pie?"

Somehow or other it seemed that even though a five-year-old American citizen couldn't speak clearly to his court-appointed captors, nevertheless he was something of a phenomenon in being able to prepare hot meals every day and otherwise manage himself and two younger children in the absence of a mother who worked two shifts—neither of them an eight-hour shift at that.

This experience was the first to remind me that it is extremely difficult to classify people into the kinds of groups that we like to construct today. The five-year-old displayed more skill than many beginning wives in their housekeeping ventures, and yet his method of communication would without question classify him as "culturally disadvantaged" or as otherwise deficient when compared with the average American five-year-old child.

In this book an attempt is made to deal with children, and specifically with preschool-age children who have various disabilities. We have not covered the "eight categories" officially recognized by the United States Office of Education (deaf, hard-of-hearing, mentally retarded, blind, etc.). The reason for this is our attempt to discuss methods and programs for children, rather than first selecting "The" child ("The" mentally retarded child, "The" deaf child, etc.) and then developing a rationale that supposedly is relevant and appropriate only for "this" child. Even so, several chapters dealing with specific disability areas are included, primarily because it is still extremely difficult to get away from the categorization process, and the chapters are relevant to the theme of the book.

This book is intended for all those interested in the general nature of preschool educational programming for children, including parents and school officials, especially those interested in the field of special education for children with disabilities.

ACKNOWLEDGMENTS

FOLLOWING MY WORK at the juvenile home in Austin, Texas, my next opportunity to work with very young children came in the Wayne Community School District in Michigan. There, Mrs. Helen Avery and I tried to undertake a screening program for kindergarteners and while we obtained some experience in the process, and in some problems, we found we had bitten off more than we could chew at the time. However, with Helen's rather inconspicuous support, we submitted a proposal and obtained a grant under the Head Start program when it was first created by the United States Office of Economic Opportunity.

In establishing our Head Start program in the Wayne schools we discovered that while at least 200 children out of the expected 2,000 kindergarten enrollments for the coming school year should be eligible, hardly any eligible candidates appeared. We sent letters to all 2,000 parents and we had stories printed in the local newspapers. But no response. Finally, we brought together the approximately fifteen teachers who were expecting summer jobs. We explained the situation to them, and worked out a plan whereby they divided up the school district and went door-to-door looking for the children. By opening day there were 200 children enrolled and while a few errors were made in selection, generally speaking the group met the criteria established by OEO.

So I want to acknowledge the Wayne Community School District, and especially Helen Avery who now holds the position of curriculum coordinator, for being interested in young children with disabilities or disadvantages.

More recently in working with the Board of Cooperative Educational Services in suburban Buffalo another group has made a significant contribution to the education of children with special problems. This group is the parents. While it seems only too obvious that the parents of children with significant problems and disabilities will be highly interested in school programs for their particular children, this group of parents seems different from most with whom we have had contact. The major difference seems to be in their effectiveness in persuading school districts to establish programs. By working carefully and skillfully with school officials there has been an increase ranging from about 30 to 100 percent each year during the past few years in the services offered to children with disabilities in the area.

At the same time, tribute must be paid to the school districts that have made a meaningful response to the needs and wishes of the parents. While a listing of names and schools may be rather tedious, I would like to take this opportunity to mention those with whom we have significant contact and who have been involved directly in our work. Undoubtedly there will be some omissions, but fear of leaving out a name does not seem reason to omit the list: Ed Allen and Al Lucia from the Akron Central School District; Wilson Conrad and Sam Trippe from the Alden Central District; John Scheller and Art Schuchardt from the Amherst Central District as well as Art York and Crede Hagerty from the Amherst Elementary Districts; Earl Boggan and Veronica Jackson from the Cheektowaga Central School District; Cliff Crooks and John O'Neil from the Clarence Central School District; Walt Heffley and Joe Gizinski from the Cleveland Hill School District; Marco Guerra and Frank Stock from the Depew School District; Vern Heiman, Marv Mandel, and Bob Starr from the Frontier Central District; Veronica Connor and Reva Kohn from the Grand Island Central School District; Harry Hatten and Bill Rodiek from the Hamburg Central School District; Tony D'Amore from the Lancaster Central School District; Sam Bennett and Frank Calzi from the Maryvale School District; Leo Kaminski from the Sloan School District; Ted Sturgis, Sid Oberacker, and Amelia Sherrets from the Sweet Home Central School District; J. Pierce McGrath, Martin Boggan, Carl Markello, and Frank Kurtz from the West Seneca Central School District, and Bill Keller and Norm Cole from the Williamsville Central School District.

ROGER REGER

CONTENTS

Preschool Programming of
Children With Disabilities

Chapter 1

INTRODUCTION

ROGER REGER

THE INTENTION OF THIS BOOK is to offer some suggestions on why preschool programs should be provided for certain children, and what facilities, equipment and materials should be provided. Also included are suggestions on how to detect problems in young children. Frequently the question is asked: "How does one know that a particular unit of behavior represents a significant problem rather than simply a 'stage' that all children experience temporarily?" Most important, some suggestions are offered on what might be done about problems once detected—recommendations are made on how an actual program might be implemented.

PHILOSOPHY

It seems that the "philosophy" of a program is of primary importance because unless it is known why a program should be established it is difficult to know exactly what kind of program to undertake. It is not enough to bring a group of children together only because somebody thinks it is "good" to have a program, or because preschool programs are "in" today, or even because of a rather naive belief that preschool programs will "prevent" all kinds of problems later. Because the prevention concept has been so widely used to justify all manner of educational and other programs more will be said later about that.

Preschool programs are important for all children because so very much happens in the first few years of life to form the kind of individual who later becomes an adult. It is only by those who think that learning to read and compute numbers are the primary concerns of school and formal education that preschool programs are held in suspicion. Some say that after all, if the purpose of going to school is to learn the three R's, and if children younger than five or six cannot learn this material, then obviously preschool programs can serve no possible purpose. Such thinking is too narrow to appreciate the purpose and reach of preschool programming.

Preschool education is important because there is so much for young children to learn, and there are so many chances for error or mistakes on the part of the parents who mean well but who simply cannot understand the full range of principles of growth and development. As a society, we recognize that almost any couple can unite and produce children. Unfortunately, we also implicitly recognize that the first few years of life are not as important as far as learning goes. Only from about age six onward, it seems, is "education" important.

Children with disabilities no less, and probably more, than children without disabilities need specialized assistance from the earliest age. Not only the children, but the parents need it as well. In fact, in most instances where problems are recognized at birth or soon after, the education of parents—as parents of a child with problems—is of utmost importance. Children who lack sensory capacities are in great need of developing skills to compensate for or overcome their disabilities. A child with a hearing loss is at a great disadvantage in learning the very, very complicated process of communication and must have specialized assistance as soon as possible.

Labels

It has been customary in the field of special education to first label children and then provide programs around the areas supposedly defined by the labels. The problem with this approach is that labels neither define nor explain and so the effect tends to be to exclude, rather than include, children from needed programs. Because some children have visual disabilities or are so difficult to manage that special assistance is needed, or have less facility with spoken language than most children, is not sufficient justification for the assumption that all children who fit into each of these problem areas must be segregated into groups and kept apart from other children.

Grouping

For some reason the belief has been successfully fostered that a child with generally retarded abilities should not associate—at least not in an educational program—with another child with hearing or visual or behavioral disabilities, or even with a "normal" child. The rationale is that the instructional needs of the children are so vastly different that nothing could be accomplished by the association of such children with each other in a formal program.

If a program is individualized, which is frequently claimed but seldom practiced, then grouping by categories becomes less important. All children have in common an ability to learn and a variety of other characteristics that are far more important than their "diagnoses" which all too often are arbitrary and irrelevant.

One very important aspect that is being ignored in the assumption of grouping by medical labels is that the most critical needs of the students relate to their existence as human beings. Children establish their own identities by comparing themselves with other children. Not only does it become important for children to establish their own identities, but as they become older and more sophisticated they must learn to recognize the existence and the identities of other children as well.

It is somewhat futile for a school district to establish a segregated special class of children—say those labeled as "mentally retarded"—and then make various peripheral efforts to have the children "integrated" and "accepted." It is almost as futile when the children become older to spend time correcting a basic error in the process by trying to get employers to "hire the mentally retarded." The fault being criticized here is not the grouping process itself, which certainly deserves some critical reviewing, but the rationale for the grouping.

Labels and Tasks

The fact is—at least it seems to us to be a fact—that medical-personal disability labels do not adequately define the task of the educator, and especially the special educator who deals specifically with problem areas. The school cannot deal with brain damage or mental retardation; the school can only deal with children who may be brain damaged or retarded. The school cannot handle the problem of deafness or blindness; it can only try to help children who may be deaf or blind to become effective persons.

This simple distinction is very important because it helps define the task of the educator. Far too many educators today do not adequately differentiate their jobs and so go about missing the mark.

The teacher who feels his task is the treatment of "the blind child" it likely to act as if this child is now and always will be in a glass case, isolated from the real world. On the other hand, the teacher who feels his task is the education of "a child who is blind" has placed the emphasis in perspective: it is the child, and not the blindness, that is of concern.

It is nothing short of tragic to see some schools and some parents place so much emphasis on irrelevant aspects of their work. Some schools insist on "producing" children who can read even though many children fall off the production line and become casualties as a result of the emphasis. This is not to say that reading is unimportant; this is only to say that no matter how important reading may be, for some children, it is a skill that must be learned in a manner different from the average. Occasionally one finds parents with a child who obviously is very disturbed and so "different" that he is noticed for his uniqueness everywhere he goes; and the parents are concerned not with helping the child overcome this great handicap but instead are shopping around for reading teachers or reading methods.

PREVENTION

One of the better arguments for funds for preschool programs is that a financial investment now will result in financial savings at a later time.

This particular argument has been used in so many places for such a long period of time it is surprising that it has never been challenged. On the surface the argument seems so self-evident that a challenge would be pointless. But it seems that the argument should be challenged not only for its accuracy from the viewpoint of its financial merits, but more importantly on philosophical grounds.

Financial Savings?

A school district that establishes preschool programs is likely to find itself spending not less, but more money on older children with problems. This is because most schools discover that as they better understand children and their problems they see a great need to do more, not less, for all children.

Sound Philosophy?

The concept of prevention as a justification for preschool programs places the emphasis on negative rather than positive factors. For example, by analogy it would be similar to saying that our comprehensive high schools today are needed because they help control delinquency, welfare costs, and unemployment—hardly a positive expression of the need for secondary programs in the public schools.

There seems little question that an effective preschool program will salvage many children who otherwise would have school years filled with misery and terror. And perhaps as a starting point this alone is sufficient reason to establish preschool programs. But a more realistic rationale should be based in positive terms such as those already mentioned.

DISABILITY AND HANDICAP

In this book a distinction is made between a disability and a handicap. A "disability" is any condition, usually as defined by social standards, that may affect an individual in a negative way across a variety of situations. A "handicap" exists only within a certain context, and may be defined by the handicapped individual, by social standards, or by certain individuals or institutions who have a position of power over the designated handicapped person.

Disability Versus Handicap

A certain disability may not be the individual's handicap. This statement can best be illustrated with an example. Let us say an individual has a visual disability, that he is partially sighted. At the same time, this individual experiences a great deal of difficulty in his day-to-day living. He (and perhaps "society in general") attributes his difficulty to his visual disability, but a moment of reflection leads one to ask why every individual with a similar visual disability does not have similar daily difficulties. A brief examination of the situation probably would reveal that the person's handicap is not his visual disability, but his lack of social skills: he simply does not know how to get along with other people and he (and/or others) blames his vision condition for his problems.

Disability Not a Handicap?

A disability may or may not be a handicap, or present a handicap to the disabled person. An ugly person has a disability but whether he is handicapped depends upon how he handles himself. Or, a person may be handicapped (say, by a hearing disability) in his social life but be as a success—nonhandicapped—in his business life. A visual or hearing loss is a disability regardless of the context; however, the sensory loss may or may not be a handicap, or it may be a handicap in some situations and not in others, and every individual with the same disability will have a different permutation of handicapping contexts.

Educational Handicap

For the purposes of this book, the preschool child with disabilities is viewed for the "educational handicap" he is likely to have. Included in educational handicap is a variety of social, family, and "academic" handicaps likely to be faced by children.

We are not actually primarily interested in the disabilities, but instead in the handicaps: the disabilities and the environments that go together to make a context where an individual either "makes it" or fails. We are especially aware that medically-defined or obvious disabilities may not be the disabilities that cause or create the handicaps. For instance, while a child may come to attention because he is blind, it may soon become obvious that his inability to get along with other children is his greatest disability as seen from the standpoint of what is likely to turn into a handicap.

FEDERAL FUNDS AND PRESCHOOL PROGRAMS

During the summer of 1968 the Board of Cooperative Educational Services submitted a proposal for a program for preschool children with disabilities for the 1968-69 school year. At the same time, to help clarify the nature of the program that should be established, a five-week program was held during the summer. This program included thirty children who were referred by local school districts. The criterion for admission was that some person (parent, school official) felt that the child will or might have a problem upon entering school at a later age. The age range for admission was two and one-half to four and one-half.

As it turned out, exactly thirty children were referred, so no child was refused admission to the summer program. The details of this program are outlined in the next chapter by Perley and Moulin (Chapter 2). The point to be made here is that if the rules established by the U. S. Office of Education were followed, only about five or six of the thirty children could be included in the program.

This point needs clarification. How could it be that of thirty children supposedly with some form of disability, only five or six would be eligible for assistance under a program financed with Federal funds? Is it possible that the thirty children did not fit the proper categories (deaf, blind, mentally retarded, etc.)? Or is it possible that the admission criterion was so "loose" that children without disabilities were enrolled?

The same situation is occurring when considering Federal funds that has occurred for many years with other types of financing. That is, only five or six of the preschool children "fit" into a single category, and Federal funds will not be approved for programs that "dump" every child into the same group—even the "nonhandicapped." Thus, in the preschool program mentioned there were several children who had visual disabilities, several with hearing disabilities, and several groups who displayed unmanageable behavior or retarded behavior. After the program terminated it was felt that two children had no problems according to the criterion.

The practical result of trying to apply the criterion established by the U. S. Office of Education would be the elimination of programs for over twenty of the children. It is true that as long as the parents were willing to shop around for physicians or school "diagnosticians" who would be willing to apply the proper labels, probably all the children would have been technically eligible for placement. However, it would have been necessary to establish approximately five different programs for the thirty children; in this instance Federal sources would not be willing or able to fund this many programs for one district, especially if a program should have only one or two children enrolled.

There is nothing new about this phenomenon. When special education programs first began they were limited for the most part to special classes for "mentally retarded" children. The criterion for admission was to somehow get through the barriers established by the school districts' psychologists. The school psychologists maintained that they were recommending for special class placement only those children who scored at or below whatever limit on intelligence scales the State Education Department mandated (usually 75 or 85 or below). In practice this never worked; the school psychologists in many states were authorized to make a "professional judgment" about whether or not a child was "mentally retarded," irrespective of his IQ. Because it is very difficult for a child to score higher than his "true score" on an intelligence scale, and because scores lower than the putative "true score" did not present the problem raised in the issue, school psychologists were in the ridiculous position of saying that a child who scored high on an intelligence scale was "mentally retarded" just so a program could be offered to the child. Thus, the so-called "professional judgment" of the school psychologist was really perverted because he was forced to say that a child who obviously was not "mentally retarded" was "mentally retarded," or face the choice of offering the child nothing at all.

The position of the Federal government is understandable. Unless funds are specifically designated for handicapped individuals, money will be spent for other programs. A current trend is for legislature to specify that a certain percentage of funds (e.g., 15% of ESEA Title III) must be spent on the handicapped.

There is no argument about the need to specifically designate funds for the handicapped. The argument is over the way "handicapped" is defined, as well as the assumption that each medically-defined group of handicapped individuals must be treated separately.

Chapter 2

A PILOT SUMMER PROGRAM

LOIS MOULIN AND SANDRA PERLEY

A FOUR-WEEK SUMMER PROGRAM was initiated by the Board of Cooperative Educational Services, First Supervisory District of Erie County, during the summer of 1968. It was intended as a pilot project for preschool children who might have difficulty when they enter school.

From an administrative viewpoint, the primary purpose of the project was to gain experience in dealing with a preschool program. Within this context, the emphasis focused upon the type of child who would be referred, the effect of the program upon him, and reactions from his parents.

Selection of the children for the program was on the basis of recommendations from participating school districts. As stated in the introductory chapter, any child who was recommended and was between two and one-half and four and one-half years of age was accepted. Names of children were given to the authors. Each family was contacted by telephone and in most cases an appointment was made for a home visit. These visits gave the teachers an opportunity to informally meet with one or both parents, observe the children, and secure necessary medical information.

The responses from the cooperating districts stated the basis for referral. Of the thirty children, one child was referred because he was blind, two of the children had a hearing loss, two were cerebral palsied, five were described as behavioral problems, six they believed had retarded general development, one child was diagnosed by a neurologist as brain damaged, one boy had a heart condition, eight were described by their parents as having unintelligible speech. Many of the children were considered to be hyperactive. Upon further observation many problems appeared to overlap. All but one child was ambulatory and three-quarters of the group were toilet-trained.

[11]

Grouping

In programming, three groups were established, each containing ten children. Each group met with the teachers for two-hour sessions twice each week. It was believed a child could function best with other children who were at similar levels of social development. Groupings were not arranged for the retarded, the brain injured, or the speech impaired. Subjective observation during the home visit and use of the PRE-SCHOOL ATTAINMENT RECORD (Doll, 1966) assisted the teachers in determining each child's level.

Location

The program was held in a centrally-located school. Ten children were supervised in one large kindergarten room by two teachers and a high school student acting as a teacher's aide. The classroom was divided into activity areas that included a large open space for free movement. Since the parents transported the children and remained at school, an additional room was used for a parent program.

THE PROGRAM

After two sessions it became apparent that the children would benefit from a program that encouraged socialization and emphasized language, speech and motor development; these became the objectives. It is generally accepted that before a child enters school, environmental experiences as well as specific developmental tasks must be mastered. It is assumed that these lay the groundwork upon which successful school achievement is built. Many of the children involved in the program did not have an adequate foundation for learning.

A schedule was designed, oriented to the needs of the children. It was believed that the youngsters would react more positively to their first "school setting" if a flexible but consistent structure was presented to foster in them a sense of security.

As each child entered he had an opportunity to choose materials to work with. The children were encouraged to verbalize and interact with their peers. At this "free time," manipulative games were presented and individual instruction given. Another area of the room was used to begin group work in developing language skills; the lesson usually lasted approximately twenty minutes. One half hour was set aside for an organized activity using finger paints, scissors, paste and other art supplies to aid in developing fine motor skills. Following this, the children washed up and sat down for a snack. This snack time was used by the teachers for informal speech games and discussing events the children had experienced. The youngsters then rested with a background of soft music. If the weather was favorable the children were taken outside and the playground equipment utilized to develop more adequate gross motor coordination. For some children it was their first experience with playground facilities. A portion of this time was used for finger plays, simple songs and games.

The materials were selected in accordance with the goals established for the program. THE PEABODY DEVELOPMENTAL LANGUAGE KIT—LEVEL P (Dunn, Horton and Smith, 1968) was the primary resource for language activities and perceptual development. With the use of its pictures, puppets and records, most of the children responded freely. Each day a lesson was introduced by the children's friend, "P. Mooney" (the puppet of motivation). Rhythm instruments as well as the Peabody kit served in helping to develop auditory discrimination and sequencing. The Society for Visual Education Pictures* aided in initiating discussions. Most of the pictures displayed reinforced the language lessons. Teaching Resource Materials† were utilized for individual instruction in the area of visual perception; with guidance from one of the teachers a child was given an opportunity to work in this area. Montessori cylinder blocks and dressing frames‡ were available; the dressing frames were large buttons, zipper, and ties. Some of the cylinder blocks varied in diameter only, while others differed in diameter and length. Many other manipulative objects such as blocks, peg boards and puzzles were among the materials the children could choose from. The use of balls and bean bags helped in developing eye-hand coordination.

THE PARENTS

It was realized that the eight-session program was a relatively short amount of time to spend with the children. Therefore, it was believed that if the parents were involved the children would then receive

---

* Society for Visual Education, Inc., Chicago, Illinois.
† Teaching Resources, Inc., 100 Boylston Street, Boston, Mass. 02116.
‡ Teaching Aids, 159 W. Kinzie Street, Chicago, Ill. 60610.

maximum benefit. The parent program gave each parent (usually the mother) an opportunity to meet informally after each session with both teachers to discuss the child's behavior and his reactions to the activities. It also gave the teacher an insight into the child's home environment. Most of the parents needed and reacted very favorably to concrete suggestions to aid them in relating with their children. Generally they benefited from the support given by the teachers. Occasionally the parents were shown films relating to child development. The sessions gave them a chance to converse with others experiencing similar problems. Three guests were invited to speak with the parents concerning different aspects of special education.

TABLE I
SPECIAL EDUCATIONAL SERVICES
Board of Cooperative Educational Services
Summer 1968
PRESCHOOL PROGRAM AT NORTH HILL ELEMENTARY SCHOOL,
MARYVALE: 26 forms returned of 29 sent

1. Generally, the quality of the program was (check one):
   Very poor   Poor   Average   7 Good   19 Excellent
2. I though my child benefited from the program (check one): (1 no response)
   Not at all   2 A little   2 Average   12 A lot   9 A great deal
3. The teachers were (check one):
   Very bad   Poor   Average   2 Good   24 Excellent
4. As far as taxpayers' money is concerned, the summer program was (check one):
   A waste   Poor use   Cost too much   6 Worthwhile
   20 Very Worthwhile
5. The length of the program (number of weeks) should be: (3 no response)
   1 4 weeks   5 weeks   1 6 weeks   7 weeks   21 8 weeks
6. The length of each school day should be (check one): (1 no response)
   Shortened   13 Remain the same   12 Lengthened

At the end of the four weeks the parents were requested to evaluate this pilot program. A check list was used with additional space for comments. The latter proved to be more insightful, and a sampling of comments follows:

"He attended nursery school last year and though it helped him somewhat, he couldn't possibly keep up with the other children. . . ."

"The education of children with learning disabilities should definitely be started at a preschool age to help this child become an acceptable member of society and to help eliminate the possibilities of emotional disturbance. . . ."

"With the help of this educational program this is the first time I can honestly say I have done something for my child besides giving him a label."

"For the first time she cares about something—her nursery school. ... The only sad thing is just as the children are reaching out to these teachers, the program is over—now where can these children turn?"

"I also enjoyed the intimate relationship between teachers and parent. It gave me a greater insight to understanding my own child better. . . ."

"I have seen such an improvement in his behavior and achievement."

"His speech improved a little, but more importantly he is speaking more freely whereas before he had very little to say."

"This program was very beneficial in starting our child to want to learn. . . ."

"These children need the opportunity to get a little head start. . . ."

OBSERVATIONS

It is unrealistic to chart and evaluate an individual's progress within such a limited amount of time, although some general observations are noteworthy. The children easily adapted to the school routine and responded positively. They entered the classroom willing to leave their parents. Several children began to verbalize more readily and to relate with their teachers and peers in a one-to-one relationship as well as in group settings. Some children who were described as management problems began to modify their behavior within the limits set for them.

At the onset of the program several children would not or were unable to sit in a chair to begin or stay with a task presented. A sequential pattern of learning needed to be initiated. This "process" began at snack time, where food was used as an incentive. At the conclusion of the program, seven children who previously did not sit in a chair, did so. There was some carry-over into other activities using no material rewards.

The parents' participation and enthusiastic response to the effect of the program upon their children suggested a need for a continuation of a program for all children who might experience difficulty in school. The teachers felt that this pilot program was beneficial in developing ideas, goals and expectations for use in organizing a pre-school program throughout the school year. Heterogenous grouping of children at this age level seemed entirely workable. Individual needs could be met with long-term planning and organization.

An elimination of handicapping labels can only broaden the scope of the program and the children reached.

REFERENCES

1. Doll, Edgar A.: *Pre-School Attainment Record,* research edition. Circle Pines, Minnesota, American Guidance Service, 1966.
2. Dunn, Lloyd M.; Horton, Kathryn B.; and Smith, James O.: *Peabody Developmental Language Kit—Level P;* Circle Pines, Minnesota, American Guidance Service.

Chapter 3

IDENTIFICATION OF PRESCHOOL CHILDREN WITH POTENTIAL LEARNING PROBLEMS

TIMOTHY ROCHFORD

DISCUSSION

CHILDREN whose academic learning difficulties are pervasive are disturbed not only in their capacity to learn but also in the area of behavior.

Most educators are well aware that learning problems are often the catalyst for negative behavior in the school. It also is an accepted fact that when individuals are placed in situations where they encounter daily frustrations they usually develop a complexity of problems.

For example, a child within the home usually has very little demand placed upon him for specific, structured learning tasks. Often it is not until the child meets the demands placed upon him in a school setting that a problem is recognized. School becomes frustrating and emotional overtones begin. Typically, the child begins to fail.

Unfortunately, many educators are indoctrinated by the "IQ bell-shaped curve concept" which indicates that some children are slow, some are fast and some are average, and therefore, "they'll always be the failures."

Holding this concept often limits educators in their acceptance of the slow or failing child, thereby stifling innovative and creative ways for help. As a result many children are often allowed to progress in school unaided and what may have begun as a relatively simple learning problem then evolves into an almost total intolerance to learning.

Knowing that children learn at different rates and to different degrees is simply not enough. We must realize that children also learn in different ways, and therefore something can and should be done.

The earliest possible identification of these children lessens the

[17]

chance of the failure process occurring while increasing the potential for remediation of the more basic problems.

Although children are often recognized as potential learning problems by their teachers as early as kindergarten, it is more promising and feasible to identify these children at an even earlier age before their problems are complicated by a variety of variables.

It is our responsibility as educators to develop an educational system that, instead of fostering a negative circle concept, would aid in alleviating it.

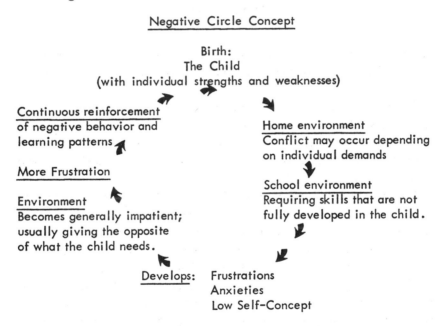

Negative Circle Concept

Birth:
The Child
(with individual strengths and weaknesses)

Continuous reinforcement
of negative behavior and
learning patterns

Home environment
Conflict may occur depending
on individual demands

More Frustration

School environment
Requiring skills that are not
fully developed in the child.

Environment
Becomes generally impatient;
usually giving the opposite
of what the child needs.

Develops: Frustrations
Anxieties
Low Self-Concept

The negative circle concept consists of a child born with a variety of strengths and weaknesses, usually with a stress upon weakness in the area that our society values—symbolic learning. (These weaknesses are usually specific, such as in the perceptual-motor areas.)

The parents who want the child to learn counting skills, names of animals, colors, and so forth in most cases can easily place this child in an anxiety-producing situation: expecting him to learn the same way as his peers or siblings. Parents become impatient and the child receives the opposite of what he needs: not patience and understanding, but anxious pushing and ridicule.

This cycle becomes even more prominent when the child is placed in school. For many children, it may occur for the first time there. Frustration and anxiety breeds more frustration and anxiety. The environment becomes more impatient; the child becomes more complex; and the cycle comes into full swing; producing an unhappy human being and frustrated future parent and citizen.

ATTEMPTS AT ALLEVIATING THE PROBLEMS: POTENTIAL SCHOOL FAILURES

An overview of our present educational system indicates that various attempts are being made to cope with the problem in the existing framework of the schools.

School systems vary greatly in their recognition of child problems, and their attempts at remediation form a wide gamut of effort and effectiveness.

The lowest "effort level" is exemplified by those school systems which do not fill even the most rudimentary individual needs of the children. Although this inability or indifference to modify their educational program may merely present an annoying obstacle to "typical" children, it can mean the difference between success and failure to children who need and often must have a modified approach to learning.

Another level is occupied by what is perhaps the current trend in dealing with the problem: the school system continues to pass children even though they were very often recognized early in their school careers as having problems. This procedure typically continues until the child cannot possibly progress any further (usually around the third or fourth grade). It is often only then that the child is "officially" labeled and placed in special classes if they exist.

It is unfortunate that approximately 85 percent of children with problems are not "officially" recognized or given appropriate help until the age of nine or ten. In an informal study of thirty children conducted by the author, 95 percent of the children who later developed learning difficulties were identified as early as kindergarten by their teachers, yet most of these children will not receive the help they need until much later. For some children, this may be too late in their school career.

While in continuous contact with youngsters in special classes for children with learning problems, a positive correlation has been noticed between early identification and help and subsequent success. The younger children usually have not developed the negative attitudes and reinforced negative learning patterns in the degree that older children have.

Data of this sort have influenced many school systems to attempt to identify and deal with the problem much earlier in the child's school career. These attempts may take the form of providing children with continuing individualized help in the regular classroom and aid by crises and/or remedial reading teachers. It also may take the form of what may be one of the most progressive attempts to deal with the problem in a regular classroom setting. Pretesting and screening of children before they can enter kindergarten and a supplementary summer program for those who show a need has become a requirement in many school systems. This initial concern and effort is often followed by readiness programs in first and second grade. In this way the schools can better adapt to and plan for the individual needs of the children.

This last example pinpoints what will hopefully become a trend in education: earlier and earlier identification of youngsters with problems so that not only the "negative circle" is stopped, but that as identification and implementation of solutions to the problem become more sophisticated, we will gain invaluable information enabling our educational system to be ultimately fitted to the child rather than the child to the system.

FUTURE TRENDS

At present only a small percentage of children with potential problems are identified at the preschool level. Even in areas where preschool programs exist, many children who need this help are not identified and given the appropriate early training.

What is needed is a system where all preschool youngsters can be screened and subsequently placed in an appropriate educational setting.

The Problem

It is necessary to look at the general framework our educational system could adopt in order to properly plan a total program for identifying and aiding preschool children who have or who exhibit potential for future learning school problems. It is not the purpose here to deal with the specific administrative techniques involved since they will be as different as the various districts involved.

It is not a question of whether to teach or not to teach preschool children, but rather of who, when, and how.

"Who" should include all children, in a natural and individualized setting;

"When" would be relative to our educational system's sophistication in working with children irrespective of age, and

"How" will depend upon the variety of characteristics exhibited by the youngsters and the willingness of our educational system to adapt to these needs.

Here will be discussed only one segment of the total preschool population: those youngsters who show potential for future problems in school. "Problems" as used here includes any factor which may inhibit the child's future growth in and adjustment to school. The child himself can, of course, be helped to a degree to adjust to the educational environment he will be facing in the future; but, beyond that degree, the schools should adapt to meet the many characteristics that cannot be modified or remediated.

Steps in Identification

Identification of preschool children who may develop learning problems constitutes a many-faceted approach. It requires:

1. A knowledge of the educational tasks that the child will be required to perform in school.

2. A breakdown of the various areas and skills (at their respective developmental levels, if known) which the child will need to accomplish required tasks.

3. A knowledge of intervening variables which have been found to affect children's school success which may occur at any stage of his development, and which may or may not occur in conjunction with weaknesses in various areas.

4. A screening method for determining and evaluating the existence and possibly the degree of the skills required and the variables which may be contributing or perhaps causative factors.

5. A setting in which educators can evaluate the effect that the degree of skills and the variables are having or may have upon the child's educational functioning. This setting should ideally have a dual role, both in an evaluative sense (as mentioned) and also in a remediative sense. It should be such as to facilitate learning in children no matter how the symptoms are manifested.

6. In order for identification to be most effective, it should reach the greatest number of children at the earliest age.

The following is suggested as an initial method for identifying preschool children who have potential for developing learning problems when placed in the present framework of our educational system.

The Setting

Ideally, school districts may develop various evaluation centers organized to screen *all* preschool youngsters on a yearly basis, beginning as early as two years or perhaps even one year. The screening should be such that specific problems would be pinpointed which may inhibit future school functioning.

The evaluation center may or may not be an extension of the school building. This, and problems such as transportation, time, segments and physical setting will again depend on the individual districts involved.

Staff

The universities are training very few people capable of filling the positions needed in this kind of setting. It would be necessary to find people who are interested in or who have had experience with children who have problems adjusting in school.

This would require professionals who are willing to look at the learning process very specifically and who have some understanding of the many implications involved in learning. They would, in a sense, be pioneers willing to explore the many facets of behavior and learning and its relationship to the school.

The staff would probably be logically divided into two areas:

1. *Screening and identifying personnel* such as the school nurse who can screen obvious medical problems such as periphereal hear-

ing and vision defects, and so forth, and evaluative personnel who can recognize the many prerequisites to academic learning and be willing to screen children in areas requiring much more depth than obvious physical defects, i.e., visual, auditory, motor areas, and environmental facets such as social, familial, and neighborhood.

2. *Teachers* who not only are continuously evaluating the children, but also would implement the techniques on a daily basis to ameliorate as many of the child's problems as possible; help the child adjust to those problems which cannot be ameliorated; and serve as a link with the school, so that the school might better adapt to the child's needs.

Both areas of personnel would be engaged in parent contact in its fullest educational implications (1) by making obvious to the parents the child's problems and the implications for both parents and child, (2) by interviewing parents to determine factors that may have direct bearing upon the child's educational adjustment, and (3) by working with parents in the educational implications of their home environment.

Evaluative Rationale

Screening or the initial identification of the children involves only a prediction of possible problems, based upon present knowledge of what is needed for success in school. The best evaluation is accomplished by actually working daily with the child in a structured setting.

Children not involved in a continuous evaluation program should return for at least yearly evaluations. Those already in the program, as mentioned earlier, will be under continuing evaluation.

Two major justifications for yearly evaluations are:

1. Problems may manifest themselves at different periods in a child's development since not only the child but his environment are in a constant state of change. Therefore, what is not a problem at age one or two may be a potential problem at age three or four.

2. Our instruments may not be sophisticated enough in some areas to find a potential problem in a child of two, but sophisticated enough to pinpoint it at age three or four.

A great deal of research is needed in the specific patterns (motor, visual, auditory, and expressive language) of growth and development in preschool children. Established norms for these growth patterns are only one of the many problems to be encountered, although there is enough current knowledge to begin appropriate preschool training.

GENERAL FRAMEWORK FOR IDENTIFICATION

Children mature physiologically and psychologically along a predictable course. Those children who lag severely in overall maturation probably will fail academically.

The basis for this immaturity (and predicted future problems) is predicated upon the use of various techniques for determining deficiencies in the motor-perceptual areas and the various environmental, psychological or social factors.

It has been found that most children who later develop problems in learning usually have deficiencies in at least some of the following areas:

Motor movements: including total body agility, balance, stiffness, limb coordination, sidedness, fine eye-hand control movements, and tactile-kinesthetic awareness of objects.

Children must learn to use their bodies in goal-directed actions. As these skills are gained, the entire body becomes a supporting and contributing action system for future interpretations and comprehensions of symbols found in the classroom.

Auditory skills: including ability to remember various sounds, to repeat them in the right order, to detect differences and similarities in sounds, to be aware of sounds in the environment, to isolate a sound from a variety of different sounds, to draw meaning from verbal direction, and to feed back various sounds.

Visual skills: including eye movements, form perception, visual memory and sequencing, visual matching, tactile-kinesthetic "feel" for form perception, and eye-hand control.

Expressive language: various evaluative techniques combining any or all of the above areas are also needed. Movement, vision, audition and verbalization must be evaluated specifically in order to determine the child's present and future functioning.

The above areas are not found in isolation and are only described here as single entities for simplification. The way a child learns involves a complex combination of the above areas. The evaluation center or schools in general should not be such that they isolate specific symptoms and then attempt to give the child an "injection" to cure each symptom he exhibits. It should be recognized, instead, that each child (even those exhibiting similar symptoms) will still need varying educational techniques in as natural a setting as possible. This setting should ideally be in a constant state of change as dictated by the needs of the child.

Environmental Problems

It is possible to evaluate a preschool youngster and find little or no signs of potential perceptual-motor problems that may inhibit future school success. Some children will be missed, and there may be those whose home environment, for a number of reasons, either causes or magnifies problems that would not exist in a more tolerable setting.

In order to identify these children, any screening device must also employ means to determine the existence of certain environmental, psychological or social factors which children with learning problems are more likely to have in common with each other.

Although it would be impossible to discuss all the various factors that might be considered, some of the more common will be discussed.

The type of home situation in which a child is reared has received much consideration. Various factors in relation to the family have been studied, including social class, parental ambition, birth order in relationship to parental expectations, family attitudes toward aggression and submission, and family disorganization. Family disorganization may take the form of family conflict, divorce, or a working mother. A combination of both divorce and a working mother, termed "double disorganization," has been cited as having a crucial impact on learning.

Other sociopsychological factors such as the child's personality (i.e., extrovert or introvert), his verbal development, his ability to interact within the home and with other social contacts, his verbal development, and techniques of family discipline all must be considered.

The evaluation center should therefore include programs geared to the child who needs growth in the social areas in order to aid future school success. Provisions for a rich manipulative environment, many opportunities for social experiences, and other enriching experiences not found in the child's home should all be made available to him.

Specific Techniques

A practical and reliable identification and screening technique should include procedures that would gather as much information as possible about the factors discussed above.

This would entail the use of evaluative techniques for determining perceptual-motor skills and a family background questionnaire and continued parental contact for providing information on the child's family environment.

Screening in itself is only the initial step in identification. At its very best, it is only able to predict those children who may have problems. It is only when children are placed in a daily educational setting that potential problems can be adequately identified and classified.

Evaluative Techniques for Determining Perceptual/Motor Skills

The author employed a self-devised test for the purpose of predicting future learning problems in four-year-olds. It was composed of thirty questions requiring the exercise of the various perceptual-motor skills already discussed as prerequisites for learning. The test also provided a section for subject comments by the tester on characteristics observed in the children.

Ninety-five percent of the predicted learning problems were later classed as such by their teachers as early as kindergarten. For example, in perceptual-motor areas, at least 85 to 90 percent of the children with predicted learning problems showed deficiencies in all of the following skills.

1. *Visual memory and sequencing:* The child was shown four pictures, for a period of one minute, in the following order: cat, dog, fish, horse. These pictures were then put away and the child received individual pictures of the same animals placed in random order upon the desk. He was then asked to put the pictures in the same order as those he had just seen with one minute allowed.

2. *Auditory memory and sequencing:* The child was instructed to listen to a series of four directions in a particular order: stand up; walk to the door; hop up and down on one foot; come back to your seat but do not sit down. A one-minute period was then allowed to elapse before he was instructed to carry out all the directions in the order they were given.

3. ***Poor speech enunciation:*** Children were asked to repeat each of the following words after they were pronounced by the tester: came, cat, barn, farm, late, lots, loan, loam.

4. ***Extremely poor gross motor control:*** A tape approximately six feet long was placed on the floor and the child was instructed to walk along it by placing one foot in front of the other. At no time was he supposed to support himself by holding on to a wall or furniture. If the child left the tape more than once, he was not given credit for this activity. The same procedure was repeated by walking backwards.

Although some of the children whose evaluations did not show potential for future problems had minor difficulty in walking backwards on the tape, every child evaluated as showing potential for future problems was unable to walk forward on the tape without either losing his balance or holding the wall or furniture for support.

Besides looking for weaknesses in the examined areas, the evaluations included comments on general characteristics exhibited by all of the children who showed potential learning problems. These included: (1) fear or hesitancy—either in coming into the testing room and/or in actually working on the test; (2) need for constant reassurance as shown by such questions as "How am I doing" and "Is this the way?", or constantly looking at the tester for visual or verbal reassurances; and (3) failure to either listen to or comprehend directions.

In viewing the test results, comments, and future observations of the kindergarten teachers, it was kept in mind that there are certain characteristics usually associated with particular age levels. Because of individual maturational differences, many children do not display the characteristics at the "typical" age but may exhibit them earlier or later. However, when these characteristics either fail to appear, become exaggerated or persist well past the typical age level, they may be viewed as symptomatic of future learning difficulties.

Family Background Questionnaire and Parental Interviews

A questionnaire of this type should ideally be geared to determine, if possible, the existence of any family and social environmental factors which have been found to influence school functioning. These factors were discussed earlier in the paper. This questionnaire, used in conjunction with close and continued parental contact, should provide needed information about the home and child and also aid in informing the parents of the educational implications of the home environment upon the child.

Educational Setting

It is only after a thorough study of the above that the child can be even tentatively identified as having the potential for future problems in school.

What might be considered the final stage of evaluation and the first step toward remediation is the child's placement in the proper educational setting within the evaluation center. This setting should ideally be geared to aiding the child in adjusting to our educational system as it presently exists, but also as a medium for exploring and discovering ways for the school to learn to adapt to children.

CONCLUSIONS

In viewing the problem of identifying children who exhibit potential for future learning problems, several important facts should be restated:

1. There is a great need to evaluate and work with all youngsters. It is only through such evaluation and experiences that educators will hopefully become more sophisticated in dealing with children at any stage of their development regardless of the problems which may exist.

2. Earlier and earlier identification of potential learning problems and proper programming offers the greatest chance for success.

3. There is a great need for standardized research on the preschool child and the implications for education.

4. As our knowledge grows, the need for the school to adapt to meet the youngster's needs and not the child continually adapting to meet the school becomes increasingly evident.

Chapter 4

EVALUATING CHILDREN

MARIAN KOPPMANN

THE DERIVATION OF IQ SCORES, percentile ranks, mental ages, language age equivalents, perceptual age equivalents, and similar scores seems to be the final product of much of the "testing" that is being done in our educational institutions today. Upon the use of these scores in many cases rests the organization of significant elements in our schools. In most school districts, classes for children who are retarded are formed on the basis of a cut off point in the range of IQ scores. In other schools some grade-level groupings, such as reading groups or even entire classes, may be organized on the basis of certain test scores.

Unfortunately once these groups have been formed the results of the testing experiences are often filed away, never again to be seen by the classroom teacher. In some school systems teachers are actually denied access to all information derived by the school psychologist or psychometrist. Although this information is generally of little help to the teacher it still seems somewhat of an affront to the professional capabilities of teachers to deny them "confidential" information about the children with whom they work each day.

Even when the results of testing are available they often are of little or no help in planning an effective program for the child in question. Since one of the functions of the school is to provide a suitable curriculum for children, it becomes necessary to examine the function of testing as it is commonly practiced in our schools. It is unusual but apparently true that after "testing," children are fitted into the existing curriculum rather than the curriculum being tailored to the needs of the children.

If preschool children are to be provided with an effective program that will do more than just prepare them for kindergarten, we must have information about the children on which to base our long-range and day-to-day planning. Present methods of reporting test results to teachers and then aiding in interpretation of these results are woefully inadequate. It is precisely because of this gap between the teacher and the "tester" (usually the school psychologist) that a need is felt for teachers to do their own testing whenever possible. This need is particularly acute at the preschool level where many of the performance and nonverbal test items are difficult to record adequately for future examination and evaluation.

There is a widespread belief among educators that looking at the results of a test will provide information about a child that will be of some help in planning academic tasks for him. Unfortunately this is not always true. The results usually tell to what degree the child was able to give the correct response. At the preschool level where the number of both verbal and nonverbal tasks the child cannot perform far exceed what he can perform, looking only at his correct responses gives only a limited amount of information. Although it is necessary to determine the child's level of functioning in a particular area, it is of far more significance to examine the kinds of mistakes the child makes.

Information is needed to determine whether the child is highly dependent on or avoids the use of any of the sense modalities in learning. This might be seen in the case of a child who, when asked to name a number of items before him, finds it necessary to hold and manipulate each of the items before responding. This might indicate that the child is highly dependent on kinesthesia in deriving information, even though the object is readily identifiable by sight.

In addition to considering the types of errors a child makes, it also is necessary to observe the process by which the child achieves his answer. The process of accomplishing educational tasks has been overlooked in our concern for the finished product or response. This may be illustrated by the child who when asked to copy several sentences from the board turns in a paper with a seemingly adequate performance. It is only through observation of the process by which he completes the task that it may be noted that he copies only one letter at a time, or must carefully consider each letter before he can remember how it is constructed, or constructs each of the letters in the wrong sequence of strokes in the wrong direction. Obviously this information is essential to any planning of the next step in this child's writing program.

If indeed it is accepted that the teacher must have the types of information that will be of the greatest help in effectively programming for the children in her class then the selection of tests will be heavily influenced in this direction. It will be desirable to use tests and testing procedures that will allow the administration of a series of tasks which can provide a basis for the observation of the child's abilities and areas of need. We have included here a few of the many tests available at the preschool and primary levels that may provide this opportunity. It cannot be overemphasized that the need for observation is of crucial importance to the understanding and effective use of these or any other tests. The sensitive and observant teacher will find that all her hours in the classroom provide an opportunity for gaining insights into and information about children which will be the basis for effective planning of educational goals and tasks.

Inventories and Profiles

These usually provide an overall look at the child, family history and general information about school readiness.

1. McGAHAN EARLY DETECTION INVENTORY (Follett Publishing Co.) assesses readiness in four areas:
   a. Social and emotional development,
   b. School readiness tasks,
   c. Motor performance, and
   d. Personal history.
It may be administered by the classroom teacher.

2. PRESCHOOL ATTAINMENT RECORD (Edgar A. Doll, research edition, American Guidance Service Inc.) appraises physical, social, and intellectual functions in young children, six months to seven years. Items in the following cases are arranged in order of increasing difficulty:
   a. Ambulation,
   b. Manipulation,
   c. Rapport,
   d. Communication,
   e. Responsibility,

f. Information,

g. Ideation, and

h. Creativity.

Assessment by both interview and observation does not require the presence of the child.

3. PREPRIMARY PROFILE (Herbert J. Schiff, Myles I. Friedman, Science Research Associates) is a rating scale based on an analysis of parents' answer given either individually or in interview, in these areas:

a. Self-sufficiency,

b. Social behavior,

c. Skill development and coordination,

d. Language and concept development, and

e. Environmental background and experience.

Language Development

Both verbal and nonverbal tests are available, each serving a slightly different need.

1. PEABODY PICTURE VOCABULARY TEST (Lloyd M. Dunn, American Guidance Service) is administered individually in ten to fifteen minutes by a teacher familiar with the procedures. No verbal response is required; the child points to one of four pictures which most closely represents the stimulus word provided by the administrator. It is for use from ages two and one-half up.

2. AMMONS FULL-RANGE PICTURE VOCABULARY TEST follows basically the same procedure as the Peabody; it uses cartoon-like drawings.

3. VERBAL LANGUAGE DEVELOPMENT SCALE (M. J. Mecham, Educational Test Bureau) is an interview method in which the "I" elicts a description from an adult informant. It is for use from birth on, untimed.

Perceptual-Motor and Integrative Tests

These give information about the development and integration of the sense modalities, especially visual.

1. ARTHUR STENCIL DESIGN TEST I gives the child the task of copying a design using stencils of different color and form

placed over one another. It is part of the Leiter International Performance Scale.

2. AYRES SPACE TEST (Jean Ayres, Western Psychological Service) is a performance test measuring spatial ability, perceptual speed, and directionality or position in space; it can be used from age three up.

3. BEERY-BUKTENICA DEVELOPMENTAL TEST OF VISUAL MOTOR INTEGRATION (Follett Publishing Co.) asks the child to draw twenty-four geometric forms which reflect coordination between visual perception and motor behavior. The forms are arranged in order of increasing difficulty.

4. FROSTIG TEST OF VISUAL PERCEPTION (Marianne Frostig, Follett Publishing Co.) may be administered individually or in small groups from age three through eight. It yields subtest scores in these areas:

    a. Eye-hand coordination,

    b. Figure-ground perception,

    c. Perceptual constancy,

    d. Position in space, and

    e. Spatial relationships.

A perceptual quotient (PQ) is also derived. Only the beginning items of each subtest are used at the preschool level.

Intelligence Tests

These are useful not for the overall score obtained but for individual subtests which may provide a situation in which to observe the child's performance in a particular area.

1. LEITER INTERNATIONAL PERFORMANCE SCALE (R. G. Leiter, Western Psychological Services) is an individual intelligence test which may be administered without language on the part of the examiner or the child. It has no time limits. It also has the advantage of the lower tests being tests of ability to learn rather than tests of acquired skills already learned. The test's sixty items include:

    a. Matching of colors and forms,

    b. Completion of patterns,

    c. Analogous designs, and

    d. Classification of objects.

2. MERRILL - PALMER PRE - SCHOOL PERFORMANCE TEST (Harcourt, Brace & World) is a battery of performance sub-tests, the majority of which depend on fine motor skills (pegboards, block designs, formboards, puzzles, tower building, etc.). A few verbal items are included dealing with the repetition of or memory for words and phrases. It is to be administered individually from twenty-four to sixty-three months.

3. MINNESOTA PRE-SCHOOL INTELLIGENCE SCALES (Western Psychological Services) is an individually administered group of twenty-six subtests consisting of thirteen verbal and thirteen nonverbal areas. It may be used from one and one-half to six years. Its verbal items include:

    a. Language comprehension,

    b. Following directions,

    c. Language facility,

    d. Vocabulary,

    e. Verbal absurdities, and

    f. Memory for objects, incomplete pictures and digits.

Its nonverbal items include:

    a. Drawing (copying, imitating),

    b. Block building,

    c. Discrimination,

    d. Recognition and tracing of forms,

    e. Puzzles,

    f. Paper folding,

    g. Recognition of omitted parts of pictures, and

    h. Imitating positions of clock hands.

Chapter 5

LANGUAGE DEVELOPMENT OF THE PRESCHOOL CHILD

WENDY SCHROEDER

THE DELAYED onset or distortion of speech development is one of the first signs of language disturbance that becomes obvious to parents of the very young preschool child. This discussion of language will begin with a definition and description of normal speech and language development, followed by suggestions for evaluation and finally suggestions for programming to stimulate speech.

WHAT IS LANGUAGE?

Language is much more than the mere articulation of verbal speech and must be differentiated if we are to observe the developmental sequence. Carroll (1963, pp. 9, 145, 149) indicates that "A structured system of verbal responses would not be a language unless it has a symbolic, communicative function." He continues with the comment that "Reading and writing at any rate, happen to be of fundamental importance in our culture and the mastery of these skills, even at a relatively simple level, multiplies the potentialities of the child for further learning and for increased self-reliance. The academic phases of school life are wholly dependent on these skills, perhaps too much dependent on them. . . . Only in rare instances is it realized that the child needs training in speaking and listening as well—that the experience and training the child gets in the family and in his general social environment do not necessarily suffice in this respect."

The interrelationship of speech with reading and writing are further emphasized with Carroll's observation that "Progress in reading depends upon progress in speech, and particularly upon vocabulary development. Oral language development should be allowed to run

[35]

ahead of reading development at all stages. . . . The influence of the home can undoubtedly be highly beneficial when parents take pains to expose the child to a suitable range of verbal experiences in meaningful contexts. . . ."

Kottmeyer (1947) states that "An oral account of an actual happening becomes in a sense a series of sound symbols for that happening and is one language step away from reality. A written or printed account of the happening becomes a symbol or series of symbols for its oral counterpart and further removed from that experience. Reading then becomes an interpreting of the written symbols of the oral symbols of an actual event."

Finally, this interrelationship of speech to reading and writing, and their interdependence upon one another is reinforced with this statement by Myklebust (1965, pp. 3, 5): "Man has a total complex of language consisting of three forms, spoken, read and written, each having a reciprocal affiliation with the other. This reciprocal, hierarchical relationship is manifested in the sequentialness of the developmental pattern." He goes on to describe the spoken aspect of language as being dependent on the integrity of auditory learning and experience. These auditory patterns, when associated with their visual equivalents, become reading. Myklebust says, "Likewise, initially learning to write entails precisely the ability to combine the visual and auditory word images."

With the preschool child we are necessarily concerned with the development of oral language. This provides the child with background that will prepare him for the further language experiences he will be exposed to as he enters kindergarten and first grade. Bond and Tinker (1967, p. 22) describe the prereading period as beginning soon after birth: "An understanding and speaking vocabulary develops gradually. In time, sentences are comprehended and properly used. As this is going on, the child develops skill in auditory and visual discrimination. Varieties of concepts are formed. Under favorable circumstances, the child develops attentive attitudes which permit listening to and comprehending of stories. If experience is extensive, if many clear concepts have been acquired, and if adequate facility in the understanding and use of language has been achieved, the child will have a distinct advantage in getting ready for reading. . . . In addition to his meeting a broad range of experiences, the child must be stimulated to discriminate sounds and objects, and to listen to and use words. It is important for older persons to talk to and with the child."

Rambusch (1962, p. 19) in discussing Montessori's views states that "The first intellectual task which confronts an infant is the requirement of spoken language. What an appalling task, the correlation of meaning with sounds. We all know that the infant does it, and that the miracle of his achievement is explicable." Again: "Montessori recognized that the young child absorbs almost all of his early learning from the environment in which he is placed. He absorbs the attitudes of his parents toward him and toward each other, without any need to recognize their adult patterns of speech. He constructs language, grammar and syntax from the environment in which he hears language used, first at the level of tonality and then at the level of meaningful speech."

Bruner (1960, p. 8) says that "The often unconscious nature of learning structures is perhaps best illustrated in learning one's own native language. Having grasped the subtle structure of a sentence, the child very rapidly learns to generate many other sentences based on this model though different in content from the original sentence learned."

As seen from the preceeding discussion of language devolpment, oral speech is related to the child's examples of speech as he hears it in his environment. Myklebust (1964) refers to this as being dependent upon the auditory modality of learning as well as environmental. Hardy (1956, p. 298) describes auditory perceptual development as beginning in the first year of a child's life, with time spent in learning how to listen. He becomes involved in the ". . . construction of a detailed pattern of conditioning and inhibition, pertinent to numerous events of sound and their meanings in his daily life, and interrelated with the rest of his sensorium." When this stage is completed, he is ready to talk. "The link between hearing and speaking is language, the mind's use of various kinds of symbols. . . . Thereafter, his symbol-making and symbol-using activities are intimately connected with the experiences of every waking hour," says Hardy.

SPEECH DEVELOPMENT

The normal development of speech begins with the birth cry. It is necessary to discuss the various stages in speech development so that parents and teachers of very young children can have a frame of reference for determining the level of functioning a particular child is on at any one time of their relationship. According to Berry and Eisenson (1956) the main stages are as follows:

1. *Reflexive vocalization:* The child cries alike to all stimuli and as such, the expression is innate and takes place without intent or awareness on the part of the infant.

2. *Babbling:* This begins at about six or seven weeks and at this time the infant shows that he is aware of the sounds he is making. If we listened to his babbling, we would note that he produces a number and variety of sounds that are greater than those contained in any given language or combinations of languages.

3. *Lalling:* The child repeats the sounds or sound combinations he hears; hearing and sound production have become associated in this very important stage.

4. *Echolalia:* During this stage the child becomes aware of sounds that others around him are making; there is no comprehension of the sounds imitated.

5. *True speech:* This development occurs sometime between the age of twelve and eighteen months, and is described as the time when the child intentionally uses the sound combinations he has been practicing and equally as important he indicates that he understands speech.

"Speech-learning, from its very inception, is a process of stimulus and response and stengthening of responses, a process in which associations are formed that are at first unintentional and meaningful" (Berry and Eisenson, 1956, p. 22). It is also important to note that unless there is satisfaction and speaking becomes something enjoyable and positive, the learning process may abruptly come to a halt. A child must feel a need to talk or he probably will not continue the practicing.

As far as the normal sequence of vocabulary development is concerned, nouns usually occur first, followed by verbs. Next is the development of adjectives and adverbs. Pronouns come as do articles, prepositions and conjunctions. As the child develops a vocabulary during the first years of language development it is not unusual to find his listening vocabulary to be far ahead of his spoken one. According to Berry and Eisenson (1956, p. 28), ". . . our mythical average child has an oral vocabulary of two or three words; by the age of two, his number of words is close to 300 and by the age of three it is almost 900. Vocabulary continues to grow very rapidly until the age of six, and somewhat less rapidly after this age."

If the parent or teacher wants to understand the maturation of various speech sounds reference can be made to a study by Poole (1934), "Genetic Development of Articulation of Consonant Sounds in Speech." A summary of the ages at which the various sounds are produced by most children is presented below:

Age in Years	*Sounds Mastered*
3½	(b), (p), (m), (w), (h)
4½	(d), (t), (n), (g), (k), (ŋ), (i)
5½	(f)
6½	(v), (ð), (ȝ), (l)
7½	(s), (ʑ), (r), (ʍ) and (θ)

Irwin (1952) states that ". . . the average baby under two months old is equipped with about seven phonemes, seven front-vowels families. At one and a half years, he has mastered the front vowels and the back consonants. Having mastered twenty-seven phonemes at two and a half years, he decelerates in the acquisition of further sounds but accelerates in the frequency of uttering his sound vocabulary. Although he begins with vowel families, after the first year his acquisition of consonants exceeds that of vowels."

Berry and Eisenson (1956, p. 84) observe that "Between the twelfth and eighteenth months, the average baby has said his first words; by the time he is two years old, he has advanced to phrases; by the age of three, he is using simple sentences. By three and a half years, practically all his responses should be comprehensible. To the extent to which the child does not maintain this time schedule, we may say that his language development is not normal." Speech also may be considered abnormal if there are deviations from the norm with respect to sound patterns, syllable patterns and word patterns. We should expect the child to articulate correctly more than 90 percent of the vowels and dipthongs by the age of two and a half, and 90 percent of the consonants by the time he is four and a half.

Gesell (1940) concludes that at age three a child's vocabulary should contain 900 to 1200 words. He should speak in well formed sentences using plurals. He should refer to himself by pronoun. At four years he should use conjunctions, understand prepositions and possess a vocabulary of 1500 words.

PROBLEMS IN SPEECH

A child whose speech has not progressed normally through the steps previously discussed and at approximately the given age for such development is often said to have "delayed speech." Berry and Eisenson (1956) describe delayed speech as:

1. A failure to appear or is late in appearance;
2. When there are deviations in the sound, syllable and word patterns so marked as to disturb the listener's ability to comprehend the patterns;
3. When vocabulary and language patterns are below the norm for one of similar age and sex.

Their discussion of the causes of delayed speech development includes:

1. Organic deficiencies and disorders such as neuromotor impairment involving the central nervous system; physiological disorders not related directly to the central nervous system such as ill health, virus disease, endocrine disorders and certain structural deviations of the speech mechanism itself such as the tongue or palate; special sensory defects as of auditory acuity, discrimination and memory;

2. Unfavorable speech environment such as lack of motivation, silent environment, poor teaching techniques, failure to identify with a loved one, unfavorable parental attitudes and personality traits, unrealistic aspiration levels, influence of siblings, twins and bilingualism;

3. Emotional disturbances in the child such as excessive emotionalism, emotional immaturity, emotional disturbances following physical trauma, negativism and autism.

TESTS OF SPEECH AND LANGUAGE

Tests appropriate for measuring the speech and language development of preschool children should begin with a routine physical examination to include a complete audiometric and visual acuity observation.

Formal tests may include the following:

1. "Developmental Sequences of Language Behavior" by A. Gesell, based on DEVELOPMENTAL DIAGNOSIS by Gesell and Amatruda, 1947.
2. PEABODY PICTURE VOCABULARY TEST by Dunn, L. M. Minneapolis, American Guidance Service, 1959.
3. ILLINOIS TEST OF PSYCHOLINGUISTIC ABILITIES by McCarthy, J. and Kirk, S. Urbana, U. of Ill., 1968.
4. WEPMAN TEST OF AUDITORY DISCRIMINATION by Wepman, J. M. Chicago, Language Research Associates, 1958.
5. A PICTURE DEEP TEST OF ARTICULATION by Mac-Donald, Eugene T. Pittsburgh, Stanwix House, 1964.
6. "Developmental Charts" in Berry and Eisenson, 1956, p. 493.
7. TEMPLIN-DARLEY TEST OF ARTICULATION: A MANUAL AND DISCUSSION OF ONE SCREENING AND DIAGNOSTIC TEST, Iowa City, Bureau of Educational Research and Service, State U. of Iowa, 1960.

PROGRAMMING AND MATERIALS

Programming for stimulation of speech and language training can be done for the enjoyment of both the preschool child and his teacher. It is important initially to help the young child listen with care and attention as this provides an opportunity to develop his auditory perception and discrimination. Frequently, children are asked to discriminate sounds around them before they have adequately been stimulated with individual sounds. It is important to build strong associations through structured stimulation before we ask them to compare. To begin this stimulation we need to introduce children to sounds and help build their awareness of them.

Suggestions for such activities may include the following:

1. Take a short walk outside or in the school building. Ask each child to listen for several sounds he hears and report them to the class upon returning.
2. Take five minutes each morning to sit in complete silence and listen for sounds (truck outside, fan, children walking in corridor, etc.). Keep a list of all sounds heard during one week.

3. Make a chart of pictures representing things that make distinctive sounds.

4. Have children draw pictures of things that make sounds.

5. Use Peabody Cards* (Level 1, B1-2-3-6-8 etc.) to identify animal sounds. Use such activities as: child making sound, child identifying sound made, associating sound and picture.

After many experiences with encouraging this awareness of sound, more specific activities may be planned to stimulate and discriminate specific gross sounds in the child's environment. Some suggestions for beginning these activities may be:

1. One vs. the other: Use instruments such as bell, whistle, harmonica, piano, etc., to present two sounds. Children must decide if they are the same or different. Activities can vary such as oral responses, coloring ditto sheets, physical responses, standing vs. sitting, and making charts.

2. Near vs. Far: Have children listen again for five minutes each day. Distinguish sounds that are near (in classroom) vs. sounds far away (outside). Using such instruments as siren, horn, etc., walk away from the children and call attention to the way the sound changes as it comes near and then fades away.

3. High vs. Low: Using such things as piano, pitch pipe, high and low whistles, bells, tonettes, etc., do activities distinguishing high and low sounds such as sorting blocks, oral responses, physical responses (sitting vs. standing), ditto sheets.

4. Loud vs. Soft: Collect pictures of things that make various sounds. Using a horn, whistle, etc., have children make loud and soft sounds—have remainder of class identify them.

5. Fast vs. Slow: Use clapping, beating drum, fast and slow music, etc., to present fast vs. slow sounds. Various activities can be used for the children to identify this difference.

As the child becomes more adept at these auditory training experiences, the teacher may begin to work with specific speech sounds. The order in which these speech sounds are introduced should follow the Poole (1934) studies' recommended ages at which the various

---

* Listed in Materials section at the end of this chapter.

consonants are produced by most children. Below is a sample series of lessons for the introduction of the "p" sound. Any sound, vowel or consonant may be substituted in the same procedure:

1. Explain how the lips are used in producing speech sounds. Used in such sounds as p, b, f, v, m;

2. Make the sound in isolation. Explain that this sound is made like a small, *quiet* explosion—lips together, build up air in the mouth and release it. Call it the "puffing sound" and have the children look in a mirror as they make it, feel the air escape as it is made. Use BIG BOOK OF SOUNDS (Flowers, 1963) for other ideas.

3. Read a story or poem with many of the sounds in each sentence. Have the child clap each time he hears the "p" sound.

4. Show pictures of things beginning with the "p" sound; one may use pictures from the PEABODY LANGUAGE DEVELOPMENT KIT.

5. Make a chart and collect pictures of things beginning the "p" sound.

6. Begin presenting orally words that do and do not begin with "p." Children must decide which words start with the "p" sound. Activities for this listening work are endless—one may use written oral responses, taking a block each time sound is heard, marking a sheet or chart each time sound is heard; clapping hands, etc.

7. Do same as in No. 6 but with sound at the end of the word.

8. Identify the presence of "p" in any position in the word.

9. Give the child a mirror and see if he can produce the sound.

THE BIG BOOK OF SOUNDS by Flowers (1963) is an excellent reference for use with the activities suggested in this section. Each consonant sound is presented in a unit containing information on how the sound is made, and with many syllable drills and word lists. Also included are jingles and poems plus sentences. These reference materials are divided into initial, medial and final position activities.

Other similar reference materials can be found in LISTENING FOR SPEECH SOUNDS by Zeder; TALKING TIME by Scott and Thompson; and CORRECTION OF DEFECTIVE CONSONANT SOUNDS by Nemoy and Davis (these are listed at the end of the chapter under "Materials").

Educational Record Sales Company (see end of chapter) sells many speech and language records that could easily be used in speech and language development programs. Some of them are:

1. "Fun with Speech," Volume I & II;
2. "First Listening Experiences;"
3. "Listen and Learn Speech Improvement," Volume I & II;
4. "Listening Time;"
5. "Listening Skills for Pre-readers," Volume I & II.

An additional listening program is published by Guidance Associates and is called LISTEN, THERE ARE SOUNDS AROUND YOU.

The Peabody Language Development Kits by Dunn, Horton and Smith are excellent programs for language stimulation experiences. Level P is designed specifically for preschool children and contains many materials and a manual with lesson plans. According to the manual (p. viii), "this level is designed primarily to stimulate the receptive, associative and expressive components of oral language development. There are listening, sequencing, rhyming, following directions and many other structured language experiences involved in this program. The Level 1 kit is basically a program for children four and a half to six and a half years of age, but there are many activities included that could be used with preschool children.

Chapter 4 in MOTORIC AIDS TO PERCEPTUAL TRAINING, by Chaney and Kephart is entitled, "Learning to Listen." This chapter gives the teacher many activities designed to help children learn how to listen. Also included are sections on sound discrimination, the association of auditory and visual commands with a motor response and auditory memory. At the end of the chapter are references for records and stories than can be used with the suggested activities.

LANGUAGE DEVELOPMENT EXPERIENCES FOR YOUNG CHILDREN by Rose Engel *et al.*, has a large section at all age levels for building oral language. LANGUAGE LOTTO by Gotkin has been developed primarily for preschool children. It consists of a series of programmed activities designed to help children develop and better understand language. There are specific areas stressing objects, prepositions, actions, objectives and relations. The Level No. 2, "Matching Pictures by Listening to Their Names," is particularly good for building auditory awareness and associations.

Level No. 3, "Verbalizing the Content of the Cards," encourages oral lanugage.

There are many additional materials available for language stimulation and production. The ones chosen to be discussed here were selected as being representative of the kinds of materials a teacher could utilize with a preschool language program. For many children, assistance in language area will need to be continued even into his early school program, As he is exposed to the visual and visual-motor areas of language such as reading and writing, his verbal development will need to be carefully structured so that necessary associations can be formed. These will include auditory-visual associations in reading, and auditory-visual-tactile-kinesthetic associations in writing. Detailed information concerning evaluation of these language areas and recommended programs for school age children can be found in SPECIAL EDUCATION: CHILDREN WITH LEARNING PROBLEMS by Reger, Schroeder and Uschold (1968).

REFERENCES

Berry, Mildred and Eisenson, Jon: *Speech Disorders: Principles and Practices of Therapy.* New York, Appleton, 1956.

Bond, Guy L., and Tinker, Miles A.: *Reading Difficulties: Their Diagnosis and Correction.* New York, Appleton, 1967.

Bruner, Jerome S.: *The Process of Education.* Cambridge, Harvard, 1960.

Carroll, John B.: *The Study of Language.* Cambridge, Harvard, 1963.

Flowers, Ann M.: *The Big Book of Sounds.* Danville, Interstate, 1963.

Gesell, A.: *The First Five Years of Life.* New York, Harper, 1940.

Gesell, A. and Armatruda, C.: *Developmental Diagnosis.* New York, Paul B. Hoeber, 1947.

Hardy, William: Problems of audition, perception, and understanding. *Volta Rev, 68,* 289, 1956.

Irwin, O. C.: Speech development in the young child: some factors related to the speech development of the infant of young child. *J Speech Hearing Dis, 17,* 269, 1952.

Kottmeyer, William: *Handbook for Remedial Reading.* St. Louis, Webster Pub. Co., 1947.

Myklebust, Helmer: *Development and Disorders of Written Language, Vol. 1, Picture Story Language Test.* New York, Grune, 1965.

Poole, Irene: Genetic development of articulation of consonant sounds in speech. *Elementary English Rev, 2,* 159, 1934.

Rambusch, Nancy M.: *Learning How to Learn.* Baltimore, Helicon, 1962.

Reger, R.; Schroeder, W.; and Uschold, K.: *Special Education: Children with Learning Problems.* New York, Oxford, 1968.

TESTS

1. Berry, Mildred and Eisenson, Jon: "Developmental Charts" in *Speech Disorders: Principles and Practices of Therapy.* New York, Appleton, 1956, Appendix 3, p. 493.

2. Dunn, L. M.: *Peabody Picture Vocabulary Test;* Minneapolis, American Guidance Service, 1959.

3. Gesell, A. and Amatruda, C.: "Developmental Sequences of Language Behavior" in *Developmental Diagnosis.* New York, Paul B. Hoeber, 1947; pp. 11-14.

4. McCarthy, J. and Kirk, S.: *Illinois Test of Psycholinguistic Abilities.* Urbana, U. of Ill., 1968.

5. McDonald, Eugene T.: *A Picture of Deep Test of Articulation.* Pittsburgh, Stanwix House, 1964.

6. *Templin-Darley Test of Articulation: A Manual and Discussion of the One Screening and Diagnostic Test.* Iowa City, Bureau of Educational Research and Service, State U. of Iowa, 1960.

7. Wepman, J. M.: *Wepman Test of Auditory Discrimination.* Chicago, Language Research Associates, 1958.

MATERIALS

1. Chaney, Clara and Kephart, Newell: *Motoric Aids to Perceptual Training.* Columbus, C. E. Merrill Pub. Co., 1968; Chapter 4, "Learning to Listen."

2. Dunn, L. M.; Horton, K. B.; and Smith, J. O.: *Peabody Language Development Kits.* American Guidance Service, Minneapolis, Minn. 55014.

3. Educational Record Sales, 157 Chambers Street, New York, N. Y. 10007:
   1. "Fun With Speech," Vol. I & II;
   2. "First Listening Experiences;"
   3. "Listen and Learn Speech Improvemnt," Vol. I & II;
   4. "Listening Time;"
   5. "Listening Skills for Pre-Readers," Vol. I & II.

4. Engle, Rose C. *et al.*: *Language Development Experiences for Young Children.* Los Angeles, Department of Exceptional Education, U. of Southern Calif., 1966.
5. Flowers, Ann M.: *The Big Book of Sounds.* Interstate Printers and Publishers, Inc.; 19-27 N. Jackson Street, Danville, Ill. 61832.
6. Gotkin, L. G.: *Language Lotto.* New York, Appleton, 1966.
7. Guidance Associates: *Listen, There are Sounds Around You.* Pleasantville, N. Y. 10570.
8. Nemoy and Davis: *Correction of Defective Consonant Sounds.* Expression Co.; P. O. Box 11, Magnolia, Mass. 01930.
9. Scott, L. and Thompson, J.: *Talking Time.* St. Louis, Webster Pub. Co.
10. Zedler, Empress: *Listening for Speech Sounds.* New York: Harper, 1955.

Chapter 6

PERCEPTUAL-MOTOR DEVELOPMENT IN THE YOUNG CHILD: PART ONE

JOAN TEACH

Perceptual-motor development is increasingly recognized as one of the vital processes involved in areas of behavior and as especially vital to the child's success in his world around him. Barsch (1967, p. 20) emphasized the need to recognize this functioning in the preschooler by stating that "within this four to five year period the human organism constructs a physical and cognitive experiential foundation for movement efficiency which will serve him throughout a lifetime." As the child exists not in a vacuum but in an interactive environment, it is important to evaluate his ability and disability to function within this framework. At the preschool level this includes especially his reaction to and knowledge of himself. He is a part of his immediate surroundings and in order to act efficiently within the environment he must know himself, his relationship to the objects in his environment and the interrelations of these objects to each other.

It has been accepted that a preschool program for young children is indeed of great benefit and value (Wylie, 1968). And so it should follow that a preschool program is necessary and essential to the child, especially if he displays a compilation of specific problems or disabilities. This chapter is designed to deal with the problems presented by children exhibiting perceptual-motor disabilities.

PERCEPTUAL MOTOR—A DISABILITY

It has long been an accepted part of the preschool curriculum to provide for the child those experiences which increase his gross or large-muscle coordination. Children are provided with slides and ladders, tunnels and blocks and are encouraged to experiment and explore. Running, skipping, hopping and jumping all become a vital and integrated part of the everyday activities of the preschooler. It is at this stage or time in a child's life that he begins to know himself. He creates an image which relates to others and how they feel. He begins through much frustration to find his own limitations. After knowing more about himself he then begins to examine his environment. He begins to see how he can fit and piece himself into the sizes and shapes of spaces in the objects around him. And, he often becomes confused and frustrated. His successful attempts outdistance his failures and learning becomes a pleasurable experience.

What happens then if a child cannot efficiently explore his world around him in a meaningful manner? What happens if what he sees and hears and feels and tastes are not properly integrated into a satisfying and meaningful whole? What if his perception is piecemeal and events, objects and situations become isolated happenings? Individual items or events each have no relationship to each other; he is completely unrelated to his surroundings. He deals with each situation as if it was presented for the first time and he never seems to learn from his past experiences.

If this is true, one can say that the child is not functioning adequately at the associative level of performance. This is the third and highest level of performance. According to Jersild (1954), a child learns first by motor movements and these are the most basic in early childhood for the creation of good mental and physical growth. From this the perceptual system is made ready and from the foundation of these two the associative system is developed. A child who is not able to perform on the associative levels must first be taught to develop the patterns and interrelationships learned through the motor and perceptual systems. A child who is unable to perform motor tasks adequately, for whom the drawing together of isolated facts and happenings is impossible, can be considered to have a perceptual-motor disability.

It is performance at this particular time that denotes his problem with no etiological suppositions of the past. Thus if a child does indeed have a problem in the development of systems prerequisite to the activities necessary to perform in school and later-life activities, one would say that a preschool program should include emphasis on the motor and motor-perceptual and perceptual-motor areas of development.

DEVELOPMENT OF THE MOTOR SYSTEM

According to embryological development, the first system to be neurologically arranged is the motor system. This is made functional before the perceptual system is ready and these first two systems are functional before the third, the associative, is laid down. In keeping with this, learnings in the human organism also begin with the motor area (Jersild, 1954; Strauss & Kephart, 1955).

The motor system has its own developmental refinements. The organism initiated control from gross movements to more specific refined movements and, from this specific refined control to complex systems of control. These systems develop in their own patterned organization by following the cephalo-caudal and the proximo-distal principles.

The cephalo-caudal principle can be explained simply by noting that the organism first differentiates the musculature in the neck area and allows movement of the head. From here it proceeds to the shoulder area. This allows the free and large movement of the arms from the shoulder socket. The next in the progression is movement to sort and separate the top and bottom halves of the trunk, the movement of the waist. Movement of the hip, leg, ankle, and toes follows in turn.

The proximo-distal principle involves the same type of progression from the center or midpoint of the body outward toward the periphery. The first infantile movements involve gross movements from the shoulder and then more specific control in the elbow. The first movement in the elbow begins in a chopping fashion and proceeds in greater control until the circular movements can be performed with perfection. The wrist moves with greater refinement of control and the fingers develop their own fine manipulations only after all of the preceeding movements are in generalized patterns.

Because of these types of progressive moving responses it should then be possible for a child to develop a vast repertoire of patterned responses which, upon meeting any situation, could be recalled. At times we find a child for whom immediate motor response is impossible. We may also find a child for whom motor movements are irratic, quick and without control. This child is able to perform some responses by means of splinter skills but cannot perform any of the related activities.

It is in recall of generalized controlled motor patterns that one notes a breakdown for the child with a perceptual-motor disability. He cannot adequately call upon more than one motor pattern with which to respond. He is often found to have only limited means of response for any one category of situations. He can neither vary the speed of the task nor can he easily change directions while he performs. He is often the child who has great difficulty starting and stopping a task. Once he begins to perform, he continues to perform until forceably stopped. As movement is requested, it is often noted that his vision is attending elsewhere and not involved in the task at all. His eyes are often seen darting from place to place not seeming to see anything long enough to gain information from it. His hearing is intent on the subtle noises about him and not on the obvious, i.e., the directions being given. This destroys the ability to gain simultaneous sensory input and leaves all learning to be gained from one sense modality at a time.

IDENTIFICATION

As with any area of disability it is always a matter of intense concern to draw the fine line that categorizes and classifies the child as definitely having or not having a particular problem. Often the educator has himself in a bind as he finds not black and white distinctions but various shades of gray. It is to this point that it seems necessary to take the positive approach.

In accepting the premise that the motor and perceptual systems of learning are developed first, at the preschool level, we then must begin to think in terms of providing experiences first on the motor and then on the early perceptual levels of development. The aspects of motor facilitation, motor-perceptual and perceptual-motor learning are true and integral parts of every nursery-age program. It is to this point that we will attempt to make observations of the preschooler's behavior and performance and help to establish a truly beneficial curriculum to aid him in his progressive development and performance.

LEVELS OF MOTOR PERFORMANCE

In order to create a meeting of the minds it is necessary to clarify the progressive order of happenings within the motor level of performance. First, one must understand how the newborn infant approaches his environment and attempts to learn from it. He moves in a nondifferentiated manner. The arms of the infant flail about with little direction or control. As time progresses, the child begins to move more and more specifically and perhaps accidentally comes in contact with his environment. The child bumps a rattle hanging in his crib. This is a simple motor movement. The experience feeds back information into the neurological system. This feedback should occur through many of the sense modalities at the same time. The tactual sense provides information about hardness and smoothness; the hearing sense that of a rattling noise; the visual sense that of red and white and round. All of these facts of learnings should then integrate themselves to provide a bank of resource information. As the child continues to experience happenings in his everyday life, the bank of information grows and grows.

As he begins to gain control over his muscles according to the cephalo-caudal and proximo-distal principles, the child finds he can, upon his own recall, create movement. He is then experiencing the "moving to learn" or motor-perception aspect of his experiences—that is to say that upon desire he can reach out and touch the rattle and collect even more information from it. This then establishes the next phase in the quest for knowledge. As time goes on the child learns that throughout specific motor output he can reach the rattle from more and more directions, including a change from back to stomach or side. He no longer has only one means of reaching the rattle and can now reach other toys as well as the rattle. After many experiences he has learned how to get himself to other items within his reach. As he rolls and squirms and wiggles, he learns that movement of the body as a whole makes more and more experience available to him.

As he generalizes more and more of his movement patterns, he can generalize more and more about the things about him in his environment. As this generalization of knowledge takes place, the child then finds out about classifications of categories and comparisons, and can then deal in aspects of perceptual-motor. The child then needs his previous backlog of information to create a foundation of what he further explores and finds out about. All of this is necessary to enable the child to perceive an object, such as a coffee cup, and understand that it is hard, possibly warm to the touch, can hold a liquid, has a smaller hole that a finger would fit into, can be emptied by tilting, can come in other colors than the one he is seeing, has other different but similar shapes and can be held. He does not need to actually hold the cup in order to know that this is true. This then is perception, the next level of performance.

INADEQUATE PERFORMANCE ON THE MOTOR LEVEL

When a child experiences a difficulty in the perceptual motor areas of performance it is not to say he does not move at all. It is to say that his methods of performance are less than optimum and often are functioning through a splinter skill and not through a good generalized and integrated performance. Society dictates many things to us and in order to survive the child finds one method of performing and continues to practice on this method whether or not the prerequisites for this movement have been established.

Walking is a good example. Many children can walk although they do not have good balance nor do they have a cross lateral crawling pattern. A child can use his walking to navigate up a pair of stairs; this is the child who steps one step at a time, pauses between steps, does not alternate right foot and then left foot but instead steps up with the left and then brings the right foot up to meet it. He seems to have one speed and shows no evidence of balance or flexibility flowing from one side of the body to the other. But, we remind ourselves, he does walk. His difficulty is seen if he must walk where balance is necessary, such as on the curbing or on a walking board. His running is often with a stiff-legged awkward gait and skipping patterns are impossible.

ADEQUATE MOTOR PERFORMANCE ON THE PRESCHOOL LEVEL

It is important to know what tasks at what level should be expected to be performed by the three-, four- or five-year-old child. Let us now explore some of the basic ways in which the child begins to learn during his preschool years (Gesell *et al.,* 1940).

Balance and Posture

Balance and the maintenance of posture is the way we establish relationship of ourselves to the world around us. It is the right-left, up-down and forward-back relationships which are only known after we have experienced them ourselves. A child should be able to maintain balance in relationship to gravity under many different postures. His balance should be dynamic and fluid and not solid and rigid. That is to say, the child should be able to "get into" and maintain balance without being as stiff as a board. He should be able to move slightly in order to keep himself in balance and should he begin to experience difficulty.

In reviewing the balancing abilities of the young child, one finds the three-year-old able to stand on one foot for a moment or so. He can tilt forward and backward and he plays with small cars and objects while he adjusts his posture from standing to sitting, kneeling and crawling. The change of posture should not interfere with the activity at hand and he frequently reverts to creeping and rolling as he plays. These are well under control and are seen in an improved sense of balance. There is very little of the sway and wobble of the toddler's gait still remaining.

By four years of age the child should be able to maintain his balance on one foot for four to eight seconds. He has improved body equilibrium and can navigate with adequate performance on the four-inch walking board, rarely having to step off with both feet to regain his balance. He performs simple tumbling stunts. There is less involvement and overflow into other areas of the body when specific activities are performed. The legs become stronger and more athletic feats are possible.

By five years of age, balance and postural adjustments should be an integral part of his life. He can stand on one foot more than eight seconds and walk the 4-inch board without stepping off. He will attempt the 2-inch walking board with difficulty. His general overall posture will give the appearance of composure and completeness.

Locomotion

The activities involved in locomotion are those of the body which propell it through space such as walking, running, jumping, skipping, hopping and rolling. It is by moving to and throughout space that the child can investigate the objects around him and through such knowledge the spatial world develops. These skills of locomotion must be flexible and varying in order to allow the child to attend to his environment and not to the process by which he moves through it.

The three-year-old has been described as being at the turning point in his young life as his massive muscles are now dominant enough to enable him to perform under control. He is nimble and sure on his feet. He can navigate corners easily and accelerate and decelerate with ease. He has facility in alternating the two sides of his body and shows these off by peddling a tricycle and walking stairs in an alternative fashion. He often responds to individual motor movements by a parallel response in the other limb. He experiments and explores in many bilateral fashions such as jumping off the bottom stairs with both feet and jumping over low obstacles.

By four years of age he is more sophisticated in his manner and way. He can run even better than the three-year-old and should easily be able to break rhythm and stride. He can broad-jump from both running and standing positions and can skip, after a fashion. He cannot hop. At this point the responses of his body are less tied together.

The five-year-old is much more self contained than the four-year-old. He finds elementary exploration involving less of his time. Because of his more mature sense of balance he moves more surely on to bigger and better things. Hopping has now become well established. Walking movements are graceful and with a keen sense of balance and agility. He has a well defined skip and can march in time to music. Upon descending stairs he can now alternate easily with little attention to his movements as such.

Eye-Hand Coordination

This category of movement begins back at the first accidental match of hand movement that caught the attention of the eye. As the patterns become sophisticated, the hand's explorations leading what the eye was seeing are taken over by the eye's wider scope now leading the hand's activities. This then leads us to the contact skills. These are the skills of the child as he reaches, grasps and finally releases an object.

The expansion of these skills are then the area of receipt and propulsion. Here the child receives a moving object from space and finally propels it back into space. These skills also include the visual pursuit of an object in space, even without any contact from other body parts. These are therefore other major information-gathering opportunities of the organism.

The three-year-old is at the brink of greater motor control. His fine musculature is becoming so developed that he is ready for exploration. He is very interested in crayon and finer manipulative play. His strokes are becoming better defined and less diffused and less repetitive. He cannot draw a man, but the movements he defines as objects are beginning to have definite characteristics and shapes. He can continue control to accomplish a tower of five or ten cubes. If carefully directed, he can fold a sheet of paper lengthwise and crosswise but cannot fold on the diagonal. At this stage, the most effective method of teaching the child is by actual demonstration.

The four-year-old experiences even finer control of the hand and sophisticated exploration of the eye. He can hurl a ball in the general direction of intent even though the point or destination is not accurate. Control of specific muscle sets enables this to be done without gross involvement of all body parts, just those inherent in good balance. He can now lace, button and snap. He can thread a large needle through well placed holes. He is more refined and precise as he begins to give attention to detail in his drawing. His drawing of a circle is executed in a clockwise direction and is more accurate than that of the three-year-old. Having to perform on the diagonal is still difficult, therefore he cannot copy the diamond or triangle although he can copy the cross. He draws a man consisting of a head and two appendages and possibly two eyes. With the blocks he constructs and labels, giving the forms created a prominent part of his dramatic play. He is curious and lively and ever ready to go on to the next challenge rather than repeat the experience.

The five-year-old shows finesse of movements in the fine motor areas as well as the gross. His ball-throwing includes a stance and the action comes from involvement of the shoulder and wrist with a cross lateral shift of body weight. He deftly thrusts pellets in a bottle, and he uses crayons with great assurance and definitiveness. He draws a man who is recognizable and his strokes show definite control. He continues to have difficulty in copying the diamond but is master of the square and triangle. In block play he can build a complicated three-dimensional structure which he defines, explains and supports.

PERFORMANCE VS. ADEQUATE PERFORMANCE

Not every three-, four- or five-year-old must be able to perform all of the tasks laid out by the preceeding levels or be considered a total failure. However, these are the very basic and necessary activities he should be able to do at this level. Being able to perform none of the activities of his age level and few at the level before would indeed suggest that the child was dealing with some type of a perceptual-motor disability. On the other hand, if there were only a few of the tasks on all levels which he could not perform, this too could indicate difficulty. It is possible that the child had learned a series of splinter skills to get him over his difficult areas.* Then too, there is always the child who defies many of the beautifully designed testing measures and still is found to have difficulties although artfully disguised.†

It is with these activities in hand that he should be able to perform so that his attempts at later learning are as positive as possible. With these experiences and abilities he can generalize and learn by drawing on his past fund of knowledge. This assures that each task is not an entirely new one. This eliminates his performing in a rigid one-shot method by splinter skills. It is with these prerequisites firmly in hand that all of the higher skills can be attempted with the best tools available. What greater reason then, for placing a developmental emphasis on the preschooler's experiences? Whether his disabilities are slightly indicated, severe, firmly established or not, it seems imperative that this type of program be presented.

---

*A splinter skill is a method of performing which has been developed to accomplish a specific task with little or no generalization to related activities.

† For further information regarding testing in these areas, see Eugene G. Roach and Newell C. Kephart: THE PURDUE PERCEPTUAL-MOTOR SURVEY. Columbus, C. E. Merrill, 1966.

(References are contained at the end of Chapter 8.)

Chapter 7

PERCEPTUAL-MOTOR DEVELOPMENT IN THE YOUNG CHILD: PART TWO

JOAN TEACH

Involving the young child in explorations and discussions of his family and friends is very basic to nursery-age programs. Another aspect is often to learn about his community and its helpers as well as many of the basic working principles in science and mathematics. These are important but we should not lose sight of the fact that the child must first begin to know himself before he can adequately relate to his surroundings.

CURRICULUM DESIGN ADDITIONS

The first and primary curricular area for the preschool child should include an intensification of the child knowing himself. This is often included in discussions of: How tall I am; How heavy: What I look like. In being aware of the perceptual-motor aspects of development, the child must learn to know about his internal self as well, not the scientific functionings of his body processes but the internal awareness of how he moves and fits into his environment. It is not enough for him to know the right and left sides of his body by name, but he must be able to have them for him in infinite patterns responding to infinite situations immediately and automatically. It is to this end that the following *Knowing-Myself Curriculum* is designed to expand and enhance the material already available.

KNOWING SELF

It is important for the child to be really aware of his various body parts. We begin by helping him explore.

This is Me

These activities increase body awareness.

1. Have the child lie on his back on a huge piece of newsprint or brown wrapping paper.
2. Trace around the outline of his body with a felt pen or dark crayon.
3. Hang the child's outline where he can stand before it.
4. Incorporate in the day's activities comments on who is taller and shorter and heavier and thinner.
5. Later, mark or label the various body parts as you talk about them.
6. Color in the clothes as you talk and explore the various body parts.

How Big, How Small

Expand the awareness of size and shape through fingerpaints. Have the child print his fingers, his hand, wrist, and explore all the movements these parts can make. They can:

1. Tiptoe on their fingertips;
2. March like giants—palms flat;
3. Move hands like a swing in the breeze;
4. Make baby's feet—print with the side of the fist and add fingertips;
5. Rock their wrists like cradles;
6. Hook two fingers together ("What can you make?"); link two other fingers together, move them both at the same time;
7. Make a print of the back of one hand and the front and see how different they are.
8. Explore with the basic shapes—circles, square, rectangle, triangle.
9. Make these shapes with any part in any position.

Explore the forearm, elbows, shoulder, knee, toes, ankles, and feet. All of these parts of your body have size and shape and they can move.

Notes on working with fingerpaints and other "messy"' media.

1. Do not avoid these areas because of the additional work and clean-up they require. Instead become aware of the additional infor-

mation this child can gain through these media. It is the child who avoids these experiences and who rebells at participating that we are most concerned about. He is the very one who can benefit most.

2. Begin by clearing the whole room, not only the immediate work area, from all extraneous materials. The room should not be supercharged with open material at any time and especially not now.

3. Arrange your spot with a good supply of newspaper on the floor around the work area. Select a spot large enough for each child to stretch his arms to full length without hitting another. It is better to work with only one or two than to involve ten who are on top of one another.

4. Place a large sheet of vinyl on the floor and tape it down securely. Use a good heavy grade to avoid tearing or buckling. Oilcloth or flooring scraps are also useful.

5. Place a good portion of the experimental material, i.e., fingerpaint, in front of each child. Allow the children to wear easily laundered old shorts and polo shirts or old pajamas. They can be brought in large paper bags and stored this way for several wearings. Learning to get dressed for the activity can be as useful as the activity itself as will be seen later.

6. The variety of experimental material used is only limited by your own imagination. A few suggestions:

    a. Fingerpaint: If the commercial variety is not available, use liquid soap and shake dry tempera paint into it. The children do their own mixing.

    b. Mix clay and water to a thin gravy consistency.

    c. Sand with and without water can be used.

    d. Flour in water mixed to a gravy paste consistency becomes more and more tacky and sticky as it is used.

    e. Salt, flour, cornstarch, all can be used dry; a wet square can be used to confine the material.

    f. To the above mix dried split peas, beans, sand and other gritty substances to increase the feeling the child experiences.

    g. Whip soap flakes and water until they look like shaving cream.

    h. Choose any of the other media that are used for relief maps or soap sculptures.

7. Let yourself become involved. It is important that you can put

your own self into the tasks to show the children the approach and encourage their own control. If you are a person who avoids this type of experience yourself, some positive thinking will go a long way. Think ahead and prepare yourself as well as the children.

8. Be original in the assortment of tasks used. The same task becomes different in different settings and when using different materials. Allow experimentation freely from the child, introduce a familiar activity, a new activity, and return to free experimentation.

9. If for any reason you wish to save a portion of the activity for the child or to use at a later time, place a single piece of construction paper over the area, and rubbing lightly you will take of a print of the child's work.

Notes on working with the child who who refuses to perform.

1. It is important to allow the child as much experimentation as possible, but his control must be maintained at the same time. As was explained earlier, only when the various sense modalities are working together is the child experiencing optimum information which can be integrated into the system. Therefore, we insist upon his watching what he is doing and working with only a moderate amount of speed. We will not allow the high speed of the hyperactive child which is explosive and uncontrolled.

2. When the hyperactive or overactive child becomes overly stimulated, restrain him firmly and emphatically. After the temper has subsided, return him immediately to the task.

3. It is not unusual for a child with a perceptual-motor disability to avoid any of these types of activities when they are presented to him. Often the parents report that this child never voluntarily puts himself into any tactually stimulating media. Therefore, when requested to put his hands or feet in wet clay silt, fingerpaint or moist sand, he immediately withdraws and often becomes upset. Avoiding the experience will not cause it to happen. Firmly grasping the child's hand and putting it through the requested activity opens up an entirely new world. Resistance may remain for the first few trials but gradually the barriers are broken down and the child finds a whole new way of finding out about his world.

Watch Me Dress

Encourage dress-up activities. It is not only important to dress one-self for mother's or teacher's sake but for himself as well. Work on dressing and undressing, especially those coats and boots so necessary in winter. Gain experience changing to clothes for painting and other play.

1. Fit into something too large. A pair of farmer's overalls are just right. The size should be such that all of us could almost fit into one. Sides and bibs should have pockets to hide things. Hem the legs so the child can stand but still have the feeling of being covered from head to toe. Mechanics' coveralls do much the same thing.

2. Wrapping—furnish aprons for the girls and chef wraps for the boys. Have them tie, button or snap. Encourage tying only for those who are very sophisticated in their fine motor control. Remember, no child is ready for the fine motor task of tying his shoes if he cannot catch and throw a ball and skip and hop and run with accurate balance, flexibility and coordination.

3. Bandages—nothing is more fun than wrapping up an accident case who needs an arm or leg bound up. Incorporate social skills as well. "How did he get hurt? How can we be more careful?" The fine motor aspect of wrapping the leg or arm encourages circular movement, twisting and turning, placing an object over and around without dropping it. When rewrapping the bandage insist on the child watching his movements Have his eyes help his hands to learn.

4. With a variety of sizes of rubbers and boots, experiment with size. "My shoe fits into this one and not this one. My hand will fit into all of these. I can fasten this one with the buckles. This one has a zipper, but it is hard. I can get in and out of this one without ever unbuckling it." Painting a white stripe on the inside along the toe, ask, "How does this pair match? Are these two a pair?"

5. Match and sort the color and size of socks. Have on hand a box of old assorted socks. "This matches this one. These are the same color but they are a different size. This one fits on my finger—it belongs to a doll. This will fit my foot, my hand, my ear, but not my elbow, head or knee." Putting your hand in a fist, ask, "How many of the socks will go over this hand?"

6. Mittens and gloves can be used in the same way.

7. Blouses and light jackets create another version. They can be put on frontwards and backwards as well as upsidedown, allowing experimentation in all varieties of positions. Allow Johnny to put his leg in the sleeve. "Where then is the rest of the blouse? Can you walk with your legs in the sleeves? Can you hop? Now Sue, you're much smaller, you try it."

Look at Me

Hang and arrange mirrors at various points around the room. Use large long mirrors in which a child can see his whole body.
1. "What is in the mirror?"
2. "Move your foot, your hand, your shoulder."
3. Pointing to a spot in the mirror, move this. "What is this?"
4. "Make a circle with your hand, your foot."
5. "Move like a donkey, fish, seal, and watch yourself."

Hang a variety of mirrors and other shiny objects at various heights along one wall:
1. "What is the mirror?"
2. "Point to that part on you. Watch the mirror."
3. "Make yourself very, very tall. What happens in the mirror?"
4. "Watch the mirror again, make yourself become very, very small. What happens now?"

(References are at the end of the next chapter.)

Chapter 8

PERCEPTUAL-MOTOR DEVELOPMENT IN THE YOUNG CHILD: PART THREE

JOAN TEACH

HOW I MOVE

Because the larger or gross muscles patterns must first be established before the finer and more minute controls take over and because we would hope to provide as many knowing experiences of movement as possible, we begin with the most basic kinds of movement a child can make, those in the area of the gross motor. It is not enough to say that we want the child just to move. The movement of the limb or body part involved must be under control at all times. Along with this control we want to see easy, fluid movement. A child should not move so fast as to eliminate control nor so slow as to seem to be feeling his way along. The overall appearance of the child should be relaxed. If an arm is to move, the rest of the body should not become overly involved. Rigidity should not be present.

I Can Tumble

Mat activities and tumbling for the preschooler are often avoided as the child seems to be playing in this manner anyway. Do not take this for granted. Provide rugs and mats to encourage movement and play along the floor. Work to create a group of movement activities into everyday tasks. Using a mat or rug have the children lie on their backs and watch the teacher. Experiment with lifting the head and smiling at the teacher, then as she calls out a limb have the child raise the limb. After the first response, move the limb in many different positions. Pause frequently to check to see who is watching. Include good visual attention in the first early stages.

From the first movements of lifting and looking add a rhythm to the movements involved. Using records, metronome, wood blocks, castanets and tambourines, have the children move to the rhythm. Note especially the child for whom movement is rapid and uncontrolled. Place your hand upon him and help him to move. Help him feel the rhythm.

Watch for overinvolvement in the rest of the body. For example, if the right arm moves there should be no great movement of the left arm of the five-year-old, although this would be more common in the three-year-old. Remembering that as a matter of development the more difficult patterns of using arm and leg on opposite sides involves crossing both axes of the body and is very difficult. These, therefore, should not be included until basic balance and basic rhythm are established.

Roll Across a Mat

Combine more and more movement. Again watch for the child who is rigid and possibly seems afraid. Help him feel what it is to roll.
1. Have him lie on his back on the mat talking to him to get him to relax.
2. Roll him over by firmly grasping his wrist and pulling him over.
3. Request that he remain relaxed and you will turn him over.
4. Once the children become accustomed to the feeling they can practice pulling each other over. For many this will be a new feeling with new sets of awareness as they move slowly through space.

Sit and Rock

Lean as far to one side as you can without toppling, and then lean to the other. Encourage imitation:
1. "Pretend you are a clock."
2. "Pretend you are a roly-poly toy."
3. "Rock the same way the doll does."
4. "Do what I do."
5. "Rock with your legs folded up Indian style, or with legs outstretched."

Directionality: Have children rock forward, backward, sidewise. Introduce the name of the direction in order to creat a definite association for the children. Help them follow a simple visual clue; paste a large red circle on a Popsickle stick. "Watch the red spot sway and rock the way it does."

Be an Animal

Imitate the walks of the various animals. Some of the more common of these are the duck, crab, kangaroo, elephant, bird. Directions for these are found in most elementary game or activity books. Don't be afraid to dream up some of your own. Add the sounds of the animals and incorporate them into story plays. Add directionality: "And the duck waddled around the pond. . . . The elephant climbed up the hill."

I Can Balance

As we explore balance, or the ability to assume a body position against the force of gravity, we begin to see that balance can be adapted to many forms. It is best to think of this in three stages— general balance in a position, balance while in motion, and regaining balance once it is lost, i.e., through space. For simplicity we will deal here with some of the primary elements of the first, balancing in a position. Later comments will deal with balance as the body is in movement.

Begin with simple body postures to be maintained over a period of time. Stand still—count to three, to five. Sit, stoop, hold.

Add less common postures and lift one part. On your hands and knees, lift one knee, lift one hand, hold. Standing, lift a leg, lean off balance. Squatting, move arms in and out.

Lift or involve more than one part. On hands and knees, lift hand and knee on one side; lift both hands; lift hand and knee on opposite sides. More than lift—complicate movement; draw a circle in the air with your hand; your knee; swing your leg right and left; straighten and bend your knee.

Involve other objects. Standing, hold a ball over your head as you swing your leg right and left. Walk along a line holding onto a broom held horizontally. Holding Indian clubs, swing right, left forward, back and alternate.

Include flexibility.

1. Bend at waist as long as you can hold and balance;
2. Bend forward, raise leg, hold;
3. Balance on your seat, legs raised, arms in front;
4. Standing, bend head to floor with hands arched;
5. Holding a ball, bend over and hold;
6. Balance on your seat with a ball between hands and legs;
7. Throw ball with feet from sitting position;
8. Crab position—lift limb, move.

From here add equipment such as beams and barrels and ropes (Mosston, 1965).

I Move Through Space

As the child begins to explore, he must be able to manipulate his body through all the various sizes and shapes about him. An obstacle course provides the best experience a child can have as it includes direction, variation and a constant adaptation of the child to space. An obstacle course by construction is a pathway through which the child can move. It can include any object which can be navigated around, under, between, through, into, or on top of, either easily or not so easily. The best advice or direction is to provide, first, the obvious and the easily understood. As the class becomes more adept at functioning with this framework demand more complicated or harder-to-perform tasks. An example is using a chair and cloth to play "tunnel." First, crawl through the tunnel and sit on the chair. Later, go around the chair like a duck, crab walk through the tunnel and slide under the chair on your tummy. Do remember that the first attempt at any new task provides the best opportunity for learning. Therefore, even though we may use the same objects from time to time, what we do with them could considerably alter the child's approach and the problem. Any variety of items can be used. A few suggestions follow.

Ladders

Laid side by side they create a path. These can also be laid on the floor with the children directed to:

1. Walk on the rungs,
2. Walk between the rungs,
3. Walk on the side supports,
4. Walk on both sides,
5. Jump over, and
6. Hop between the rungs.

They can be propped on stands, leaned or fastened against the wall to climb, or propped up on end and fastened. Place a mat under all areas where falls could possibly occur and fasten all raised areas securely.

Boxes

Many furniture and appliance stores will be only too happy to drop off used cartons when they are making deliveries in your vicinity. Taking an appliance (i.e., washer) box, cut several sizes and shapes of holes in the sides. Begin with the more basic shapes—circle, square, rectangle, triangle, diamond. Have the children go in one, the square, and out the other, the circle. Include color by painting the sides various colors.

Cut out sheets: Use the longer and thinner boxes or single sheets or sides of boxes. Cut holes that may not fit the whole body. Set this up similar to a divider or cubicle shield, with:

1. a circle that a head but not the shoulders would fit into;
2. a triangle that would fit a foot or hand, but not a head, and
3. a diamond only large enough for a small "pinky" finger.

Have the children go through the larger shapes backward, go through blindfolded, and—on the cut out sheet—find the diamond; the circle; the triangle while blindfolded.

Chairs

As they are commonly available in a variety of shapes and sizes, use chairs freely to your advantage. A chair does not always have to be upright, it can also be laid on its side, back, or upside down. The legs and seat form a natural bridge. The legs and arms may also be used as barriers to reach through. These are limited only by your own creativity.

Ropes

Because of their lack of formal design, they can be used for everything from a barrier, to a path, to an interesting design to follow:

1. Casually drop the rope in a snake. Have the children hop in and out of the coils using two feet and then one foot.
2. String the rope on poles for runways or alleys.
3. Wind the rope through a maze of tables and chair legs.
4. Follow the rope and go where it goes.
5. Hold the rope at varying heights. Jump over, hop over.
6. Gently swing the rope. Jump over, hop over.
7. Rippling the rope, crawl under, jump through.

More ordinary jumping with rope takes a very skilled and coordinated youngster and at this age is to be avoided.

Tunnels

These can be purchased, made out of fabric covering a huge wire coil or come as hard tubes. It is not necessary to have a tunnel to "tunnel." Obtain more cardboard cartons. If a large long (i.e., hot water heater) box is not available, tape several together. Arch chairs in a line and drape over a bedspread, curtain or rug. Some segmented gym mats can be rolled. Two long and high piles of blocks with or without a "roof" make a tunnel. A child can crawl through the legs of a line of children, or have the group kneel and place their hands on the floor making an arch.

Paths

These can be made rather formally or just constructed by symbols or words. One method is to paint or tape a line to follow. Tempera washes off easily from most smooth surfaces. Vary the width of line, make it as dashed lines, spots. Assign each foot a color. Follow the spots or lines with each foot. Another method is to follow the rope, string, cord or yarn. Using a variety of color, string several paths. Each child is to follow his own color. It is often necessary to give him his "color" to carry with him as a clue for the first trials. Cut around paper shapes and tape them to the floor to play animal twister. Tell a story including the animals. Each child is an animal and follows the various paths. Or using one path, they change animals as their animal path changes. Provide sign posts—through visual clues, give directions at various points with arrows, stick figures to imitate, animals, letters to imitate, etc.

Balancing

As has been discussed earlier, basic balance and flexibility are needed as a background for all other activity. Therefore balance is incorporated as a very necessary part of the obstacle area also.

Wood blocks: Just stepping upon a raised object can be difficult for some. Include this task by instructing them to: step over, walk around, stand on and hold, and jump over (adjust to size of the block). If a child has difficulty just stepping up he may first need more activities in the simple areas of balance (see earlier suggestions on balance).

Walking board: Use a 2-inch by 4-inch board propped upon standards. Remember the various skill levels of the preschooler and work for navigation of the 4-inch side. Instruct the children to walk frontward, backward, sidewise; walk slowly, more quickly; carry various weights of objects across the board; walk any similarly raised objects—curbs, fences, sandbox rims, walls. Put several boards together in a pattern and have the children walk between them, walk one foot on each board, walk with one on an angle, hop over and crawl under the boards.

Balance boards: As balance increases, the child can maintain his balance on a 12-inch square supported by just a post. This short distance requires a constant survey on control or the board tilts from one side to the other. Any object which insists that the child begin to balance can be used. Even the floor with a line to follow can be established as a balancing task.

Springing and Jumping Objects

In order to increase his flexibility and balance, the child should experience times of freedom in movement through space. Therefore, we want to include a variety of springing, bouncing and jumping tasks. If space is available, an old set of springs and mattress can be kept in a corner. Usually space is more limited and a device such as the

Spring-O-lene is more practical. This is composed of two sheets of plywood with heavy springs placed between the layers. A springing plank is a long plank about 10 to 12 inches wide with 1-inch holes drilled along the midline and securely fastened to standards at the ends. The plank will spring as the child walks, is wide enough for crawling and will also support jumping and hopping.

Shoe springs or jumping shoes: Individuals can experiment with springs which fasten onto their own shoes.

Jumping tires: Large innertubes covered with canvas are excellent as individual jumping devices. Tires and innertubes can be used in infinite variety to aid balance by walking on them or spatial adjustment by crawling through them.

Pogo sticks and stilts: Both of these are basically beyond the skills of the preschooler.

Trampoline: Few of these are readily available for preschool groups. Begin with the same types of activities one would use if on the ground for balance and begin to vibrate the bed as the child maintains balance. Progress then to a simple jump and seat drop. Be sure to use all of the normal safety precautions suggested for trampoline use (Chaney & Kephart, 1968; Kephart, 1960, Mosston, 1965).

Safety precautions should be taken with any equipment used. Mats should be placed under most of this type of equipment and spotters should be used.

I Can Play

Ball play is a fine method of creating a real match between eye and hand for the child. This matching must take place to sophisticate the eye control so it then leads the activity of the hand.

Large Balls

Begin with the largest balls you can find—the child must feel and see at the same time. A large ball such as a beach ball will have to be caught with two hands and the size and color is such that it is not apt to be missed.

1. Throw slowly and directly to the children in a group.
2. Throw deliberately to the right, left, high and low. Insist upon catching with two hands.

3. Throw to each other—a great variety must now exist.
4. Include body parts, possibly those printed in plaster of paris earlier in the day—hit it back with a knee, toe, elbow.
5. Try adaptations of dodge ball.
6. On your tummy, tap the ball back with your shoulder, head. Watch as those without control may miss and connect with the floor instead.

Balloons

Any ball play can also be done with balloons; the pace is slower. Buoyancy enables you to hit it with your nose, shoulder, etc. Call out a child's name and body part. Balloons can also be blown back and forth across a line by two teams. Tap balloons through limits or holes. Increase control.

Smaller Balls

Catching and throwing becomes a new game with the different sized ball. Throw at an object and knock it down; Throw through an opening; and suspend the ball from a wire or string to be hit with a body part, a stick (extension), a stick held with both hands (mark).

Any ball play can also be done with balloons; the pace is slower.

Again, there is no limit to the variety of individual tasks that can be performed with a collection of balls and a little ingenuity. It is not the task in its directions that is so important, but the matching and integration of the various senses that takes place.

This leads us to the final curriculum addition, that of the fine motor, eye-hand coordination.

What I Can Do for Myself

As the child peers into his adult-infested world he sees more and more of the sophisticated and intricate tasks that the older persons around him can perform. If he is having trouble it is these very tasks that he will practice until he can accomplish them, a splintered performance. This last area of consideration is placed in such an order that the child should in his finer motor control be able to accomplish the earlier ones first, and then later and later tasks to finer control. All school-related tasks have been carefully avoided as it is the prerequisites developed in the preschool years that concern us.

Manipulative Play

This area has been discussed somewhat earlier in light of some of the things that could be done with fingerpainting.

Fingerpainting: Any of the expressive movements that could be made by any body part.

Clay: Have the children form pinching and poking holes in the clay. Use a good sized piece for each child, at least an adult handful. It is important that the young child has enough to work with both hands. Encourage form out of the lump.

Sand table: The children can build castles and trenches and caves. Encourage social interaction and story play.

Water play: In a water table the children can play with floating objects carefully placed, dunking and surfacing, and moving objects with water waves not touching the toy.

Early Reach, Grasp and Release

Before a pencil can be held and used as a writing tool, the children must be able to accurately focus the eyes in relation to the hand and grasp the instrument.

Blocks: Use first the larger blocks of pasteboard or wood. These can create objects large enough to crawl into, around, etc. Also have the smaller wooden set available for experimentation play. "You build, can he copy?" "Can one child build and have his friend copy?"

Cars and trucks: For both boys and girls, various sizes of cars and trucks can provide good stimulative play. One finds the child crawling and creeping, rolling and leaning as he runs his charge through imaginary roads and avenues.

Tea sets and doll corners: Again an experience in socialization and interaction the child reflects and expresses. Expand this then to experiencing handling and playing with all of the miniature sizes of objects he sees everyday.

Puzzles: Begin with the one-piece puzzles, and then expand to two- and three-piece objects. Include puzzles where one object is presented in a progression of sizes. Advance to more complicated, several-part figures.

Pegboards: Little direction has to be insisted upon at this age.

Have an assortment of pegs or golf tees and a good size regular holed ceiling tile. Peg-town is an expansion of this with trees, houses and cars, all with a peg extension. Streets are so placed as to create any number of variety.

Large Eye-Hand Control

Paint and brushes: Using the large No. 10 brush, the children can paint on huge sheets of newsprint hung from easels, placed flat on the floor or spread across a large low table. Experiment with any kind of free form and encourage the child to tell about his product. In encouraging painting to limits have children paint inside box lids, on top of box lids, and inside cut-out forms. Use any of these in later projects. It is important for the child to learn how to control to a limit. The actual limits can be felt in these activiites. Also encourage the children to paint inside free forms—fill them in, scribble drawings, paint in what shapes they see, and create basic forms on their own.

Chalkboard: Experiment with large free movements. Experiment with copying and tracing. Use limits and encourage control. Introduce circles with one hand, two hands. Body alignment must remain stable.

Tying

This is the finest and most minute area of control and should be left to only the most advanced (Ebersole, 1968).

With the ideas put forth in these chapters, it is recommended that all preschool programs follow a decided emphasis on perceptual-motor development in order to best prepare all children for the world of learning inside the school doors.

REFERENCES

1. Barsch, Ray H.: *Achieving Perceptual-Motor Efficiency.* Seattle, Special Child Publications, 1967.
2. Chaney, Clara M., and Kephart, Newell C.: *Motoric Aids to Perceptual Training.* Columbus, C. E. Merrill, 1968.
3. Ebersole, Marylou; Kephart, Newell C.; and Ebersole, James B.: *Steps to Achievement for the Slow Learner.* Columbus, C. E. Merrill, 1968.

4. Gesell, Arnold, *et al.*: *The First Five Years of Life.* New York and London: Harper, 1940.

5. Jersild, A. T.: *Child Psychology.* Englewood Cliffs, Prentice-Hall, 1954.

6. Kephart, Newell C.: *The Slow Learner in the Classroom.* Columbus, C. E. Merrill, 1960.

7. Mosston, Muska: *Developmental Movement.* Columbus, C. E. Merrill, 1965.

8. Roach, Eugene, and Kephart, Newell C.: *The Purdue Perceptual-Motor Survey.* Columbus, C. E. Merrill, 1966.

9. Strauss, A. S. and Kephart, N. C.: *Psychopathology and Education of the Brain-Injured Child.* New York, Grune, 1955, vol. II.

10. Wylie, Joanne: *A Creative Guide for Pre-School Teachers.* Chicago, Western Pub. Co., 1968.

Chapter 9

AN APPROACH TO MATERIALS FOR
THE PRESCHOOLER

SUSANNE ROBERTS

For CHILDREN TO establish their own identities they must have some basis for comparison. They must compare themselves to other children. To compare, to develop their self-images and to relate to their existence as human beings to the world around them, children interact with other children.

Schoolage children are surrounded by an atmosphere that forces comparison all day, fostering a kind of identity-finding, depending upon the children they are relating to and identifying with. Thus one can find in many special school programs hard-of-hearing school children identifying and forming the behavior patterns of deaf children; partially-sighted children identifying as blind children; children with physical disabilities being taught as handicapped children and so developing handicapped behaviors.

But what about the preschool child? To whom and what does he relate? What are his frames of reference for establishing an identity?

For the most part preschool children first relate to the family and siblings and then to the neighborhood. The neighborhood is the preschool child's "school," the block his "classroom." Preschool children must therefore establish their identities by comparing themselves to other neighborhood children—their "classmates." What the preschool child learns, the tools and social skills he acquires are dependent on his experiences within his home and neighborhood. The social skills and experiences of each preschool child will thus vary greatly depending on the atmosphere of the home and the neighborhood. What they have to offer to the child, what restrictions or freedoms and the degree to which they offer the child a rich and varied set of experiences will then be reflected in the degree to which a child has established his identity and can relate this in turn to those about him.

A child in an isolated rural area will have limited social experience compared to a child in a suburban subdevelopment and they both will have different experiences from those of a child growing up on a tenement block. However children from those three neighborhoods could move into the same block at the age of three or four and through common experience, friendship, play and the sharing between them of the knowledge their previous environments have already given them, they can become people sharing, relating as individuals and as a unit, cohesively without "handicapping influences," learning together and sharing together, each offering to the group his unique experiences and knowledge.

And so what should keep a child who does not hear as well as some children from joining a game of hide-and-seek with a boy who has never been in a cornfield or with a girl who has never ridden on a subway train? A partially-sighted child should roller-skate as well as his neighborhood peers, a child who uses crutches can puddle about a tot swimming pool with the rest of the children. For small children there are no sandboxes for the partially-sighted, sledding hills for the mentally retarded or swimming pools for the deaf.

It is therefore important to go into the neighborhood and look at children, look at what they are doing together before they are labeled by schools and educators. Go to the homes and yards and playgrounds and see what preschool children use in their play and "work." It can be here that the best "materials" and learning experiences can be discovered for use in preschool programs for children with any and/or all disabilities. What helps to bring preschool children together—what common games, toys, objects, rituals, play areas, what experiences do children use in the neighborhood to learn with, to grow with before they come to school?

When watching preschool children at play it very soon becomes apparent the importance that make-believe has in their play and interactions. A field of tall grass becomes a jungle, a drainage ditch a river, an old shed a castle, an abandoned car a spaceship. Also apparent is that a classroom or a school cannot provide children with a field of grass, a tree to climb, an old garage, a coal bin or a deserted car. But because "secret places" and corners to stir the imagination are essential in the development of the young child, good substitutes should be provided.

Teaching Aids, a division of A. Daigger and Co., manufactures a three sided Hardwood Playhouse (16)* that can be put to many effective uses; it becomes a fort, a gingerbread house, or a castle. The same company manufactures compact Chair Blocks (9), ordered in pairs, that can be used as a doll's bed, the engine and cars of a train, a set of shelves or a cave. For the playground, Teacher Aids manufactures a Pole Tree (26) that can challenge any would-be Tarzan; the Rimp Romp (30) is a contoured shape that can become a horse, a camel or a big bird to the child using it. Meadow Mushrooms (20) in three sizes can be permanent chairs and tables or giant stepping stones to a great adventure. All of the playground items are made of steel reinforced concrete.

Hammett's distributes a set of thirty-three Blockbuster Building Boards (4) that can be used to construct tunnels, stores, barns and houses. Along this same line, they also distribute a nursery set of Unit Building Blocks (37) (fourteen shapes for fifteen children) and Brick (look-alike) Blockbuster Blocks (3).

Children also transport themselves out of their surroundings by dressing up—acting out—being a different person. Putting on mother's dress and high-heeled shoes can make a little girl a movie star. An oversized leather jacket and a holster can make a four-year-old a cattle rustler.

Instructo has introduced a new dimension to durable classroom costuming and, leading to that, an opportunity for creative dramatics with their Puppet Playmates (28). Made of laminated washable craft board, the die cut arm and head holes comfortably fit any young child. These craftboard "characters" come in five sets: The Three Pigs, Space Explorers, Community Helpers, Original Story Characters, and Goldilocks and The Three Bears.

Imagination also can be stirred and creative play encouraged through the use of puppets and puppet theatres. Hammett's distributes a Puppet Stage (29) (27 in. wide, 26 in. high, 12 in. deep) and many Puppet Sets. They have a set of Puppet Community Helpers (8), Family Hand Puppets (14) and Steiff Animal Puppets (34).

---

*In this chapter and the next, sources of materials are referred to by number and are listed at the end of each chapter. Addresses of the companies are listed at the end of each chapter.

To further stimulate imaginative interaction between the children and to encourage socializing play, many of the typical children's toys should be made available to the children. Trucks, trains, and boats; a sandbox and sandtable (indoors and out); dolls, doll buggies, clothes, a doll house, a toy gas station, ranch set, and airport models all delight children and encourage activity.

Imitation can be flattering or disconcerting to adults. Imitation among children is usually disconcerting to many adults. But this imitation among preschool children, of the adults around them, is essential to the development of future roles the children must grow to play and work in. Housekeeping toys such as a toy refrigerator and stove, sink equipped with toy pots and pans, dishes and silver, a broom, mop and dustpan, acquaint the child with "tools" they will use all their lives and will help them to familiarize themselves with everyday objects. Teaching Aids and Hammett's distribute many items in the housekeeping line (1, 18). Children also like using their father's tools (to the dismay of many fathers). An elementary workbench (13) supplied with small simple tools or construction toys, such as Tinkertoys (36), Mechanics Bench (21), Bolt-It (5), and Bolts and Nuts (6), can satisfy the do-it-yourself urge in young children.

Going beyond play or more accurately combining play with more concrete learning concepts, a program for the preschool child should be supplied with manipulative devices. Some "toys" that can be used to develop motor coordination and general muscular coordination are: The Old Woman Laced in a Shoe (22) to promote shoe tying and lacing; Jumbo Beads (17) to string; Parquetry Blocks (23), Pounding Bench (27), Coordination Board (10), and the Sifo Beginner's Inlay Puzzles (2). Teaching Aids distributes toys that encourage children to learn size discrimination, based on Montessori principles (7, 19, 25). Also based on Montessori principles, Teaching Aids has Sound Boxes (32) to encourage listening discrimination and Thermal Cylinders (35) to help children become skilled in thermal discrimination. To further sound and rhythm development, rhythm band instruments are fun and a delight to children. There are many sets available and guides to songs and programs for preschool children (12, 31).

Taking a look at actual teaching materials, Perley and Moulin in Chapter 2 report that an essential and integral part of their preschool program was the PEABODY LANGUAGE KIT NO. 1 (24). They used it in developing listening, speaking and communication skills through the use of the kit's color chips, puppets and pictures.

Records can also be used to develop listening discrimination. Scott, Foresman and Company has available a set of four records, with forty-two pictures and three charts, called SOUNDS I CAN HEAR (33).

Many more materials with multiple uses and approaches are listed in the following few pages. With the establishment of Federally-funded instructional materials centers for exceptional education and the ever-increasing interest in all areas of special education, many resources are available to the educator innovating preschool programs. Head Start has also focused attention on the preschool child and the importance of development of that age. But more important than sophisticated furnishings and materials is the philosophy and use of these materials with the child. The child is the most important "material" that is to be worked with, not the books and records, toys and furniture.

The program should be child-centered, not material-centered. The supplies and materials are available for the child, not the child for the supplies and materials. Referring again to the "neighborhood" view of thinking, the approach to the use of any or all materials in any program that deals with many kinds of children should be only what interests and what benefits the child from his point of view. As educators there should always be the realization that it is the child and how he views himself that is the prime concern in any educational program. The job to be done is then to adjust each learning situation so that the child views himself and his ability at the best, the optimum level of achievement that particular child is capable of, despite any disability or disadvantage.

MATERIALS FOR THE PRESCHOOLER

Item	Distributor	Price
1. Aluminum Pots and Pans (6 pieces)	J. L. Hammett Co.	$8.50
2. Beginner's Inlay Puzzles (Sifo)	J. L. Hammett Co.	$1.80 ea.
3. Blockbuster Blocks	J. L. Hammett Co.	$6.25 set
4. Blockbuster Building Boards (set of 33)	J. L. Hammett Co.	$8.25
5. Bolt-It	J. L. Hammett Co.	$2.25

Item	Distributor	Price
6. Bolts 'n' Nuts	J. L. Hammett Co.	$3.00
7. (The) Broad Stair (more difficult size discrimination)	Teaching Aids	$14.95
8. Community Workers (Puppets, white and/or Negro)	J. L. Hammett Co.	$6.00
9. Compact Chair Blocks	Teaching Aids	$15.75 per pair
10. Coordination Board	J. L. Hammett Co.	$2.00
11. Dressing Frames (set of eight)	Teaching Aids	$4.50 per frame
12. Economy of Rhythm Band Set (for 15 children)	J. L. Hammett Co.	$13.50
13. Elementary Size Workbench	Beckley-Cardy	$42.90
14. Family Hand Puppets (white and/or Negro)	J. L. Hammett Co.	$7.50
15. Hammett's Hollow Blocks (nursery set)	J. L. Hammett Co.	$107.50
16. Hardwood Playhouse (3 side—4 × 4 × 4 ft.)	Teaching Aids	$69.95
17. Jumbo Beads (Playskool)	J. L. Hammett Co.	$1.75
18. Kitchen Equipment Set (sink, stove, refrigerator, cabinet, washer, dryer, 28-36 in. high)	Teaching Aids	$162.75 (wood) $66.00 (metal)
19. (The) Long Stair (size discrimination blocks)	Teaching Aids	$11.50
20. Meadow Mushrooms	Teaching Aids	$84.00 (mammoth) $69.00 (medium) $39.00 (midget)
21. Mechanics Bench	J. L. Hammett Co.	$2.00
22. (The) Old Woman Laced in a Shoe (Sifo)	J. L. Hammett Co.	$3.75
23. Parquetry Blocks	J. L. Hammett Co.	$2.25
24. PEABODY LANGUAGE DEVELOPMENT KIT, LEV. P	American Guidance	$52.00
25. Pink Tower (size discrimination blocks)	Teaching Aids	$13.50
26. Pole Tree	Teaching Aids	$296.00
27. Pounding Bench (Playskool)	J. L. Hammett Co.	$3.50
28. Puppet Playmates (Instructo)	J. L. Hammett Co.	$4.95 set
29. Puppet Stage	J. L. Hammett Co.	$17.00
30. Rimp Romp	Teaching Aids	$97.00
31. SONGS FOR NURSERY SCHOOL	J. L. Hammett Co.	$3.95
32. Sound Boxes	Teaching Aids	$18.00
33. SOUNDS I CAN HEAR	Scott, Foresman	$15.00
34. Steiff Animal Puppets (monkey, rabbit, frog, lion, cocker, tiger, squirrel)	J. L. Hammett Co.	$5.50-$6.75
35. Thermal Cylinders	Teaching Aids	$17.85
36. Tinkertoys (Big Boy)	J. L. Hammett Co.	$5.50
37. Unit Building Blocks (Nursery set 14 shapes for 15 children)	J. L. Hammett Co.	$117.00

DISTRIBUTORS

1. American Guidance Service, Inc., Publisher's Building, Circle Pines, Minn. 55014.
2. Beckley-Cardy Co., 1900 N. Narragansett Avenue, Chicago, Ill. 60639.
3. J. L. Hammett Co., 165 Water Street, Lyons, N. Y. 14489.
4. Scott, Foresman and Co., Glenview, Ill.
5. Teaching Aids Division, A. Daigger and Co., 159 W. Kenzie Street, Chicago, Ill. 60610.

Chapter 10

A TEACHER'S REFERENCE TO PRESCHOOL MATERIALS

NANCY DETRICK

As NOTED BY Miss Roberts in the previous chapter, preschool education exists not to replace the home but to enrich a child's first experiences with the world around him. This task requires trained teachers with patience and understanding of the preschool child's needs. The teacher must create an enriched curriculum that will stimulate the child's imaginative, creative, and intellectual curiosity. With this in mind, the teacher should involve the child with stories and picture books, painting and clay modeling, observation of nature and pets, science activities, singing, dancing, and rhythms, block building, games, and simple excursions outside of the school.

Many of the art materials necessary for planning a preschool program can be purchased relatively inexpensively through the Milton Bradley Company (16). This particular company offers crayons, both wax and semi-pressed, in a wide variety of sizes and colors; poster paint, a high quality paint available in both liquid and powdered forms in many colors; finger paints, also available in liquid and powdered forms; paper, which includes all-purpose paper, construction paper, and poster paper, all in a large variety of brilliant colors; Adhezo paste, a creamy white multi-surface paste; modeling clay, a soft clay easily molded by even the smallest hands; and a color wheel, for the teaching of color-mixing and color harmony.

Other preschool materials offered by the Milton Bradley Company are: large beads and laces of different shapes and colors that aid the child in understanding the common quantity in groups of the same number and leads to many stringing and counting experiences. Toy money teaches the child the value of paper money and coins; parquetry design blocks are an aid in training the young child to see likenesses

[83]

and differences; paper dolls through play teach the child about dressing himself; sewing cards develop the child's coordination and ability to concentrate. Tiny Tot Puzzles are a child's first puzzle; cubical counting blocks are for work with counting and groups; Ring Toss is a game to develop manual dexterity and coordination in playing; Jolly Time Dominoes teach children how to match pictures that are alike; Spin 'n' Color teaches a child with a spin to determine who colors and where. Other materials are Play with Felts, a wide variety of felt shapes in six colors for creative designs; a day-by-day calendar for teaching months and days of the week; number concepts cards, clearly defined pictures and patterns for aid in recognizing numbers; alphabet wall cards for learning the alphabet; cardboard letters, for "feeling" the letters; and flannel board materials available in a wide variety of shapes and sizes.

In order to learn to read successfully children first must learn how to listen, develop visual discrimination, acquire a background of concepts and experiences with literature, know how to follow directions, and learn to express themselves orally.

These principles are thoroughly developed in Allyn and Bacon's (2) modern reading readiness program OUR BOOK. The program was developed by Marion Atwood, formerly supervisor of the primary grades at Milton Academy in Massachusetts. The program consists of the following materials which may be purchased separately or as a complete unit: Our Book Easel, bound so that it can be opened and closed like an ordinary book; Cut-outs, approximately 350 cutouts represent toys, tea party, transportation, shapes and colors, nursery rhymes, symbols for marking colors, and crayons; Pictures, a set of twelve; spirit masters, for worksheets; and a teacher's manual, complete lesson-by-lesson plans and materials needed for each lesson.

New materials from Scott, Foresman and Company (24) for a preschool program consist of SOUNDS I CAN HEAR, a four-volume set of records and visual aids divided into these categories: "Sounds Around the House," "Sounds Around the Farm in the Zoo," "Sounds Around the Neighborhood," "Games with Sounds," and "Sounds Around the School." These listening experiences and a host of others motivate children to keep their ears tuned in. The sharpening of auditory discrimination becomes effective and enjoyable.

Picture cards accompanying each album are full-color photographs of the persons, animals, and objects heard on the records. There are also large picture charts that bring the picture card photographs together in their appropriate setting—home, zoo-farm, and neighborhood.

Also from Scott, Foresman and Company is MATCH-AND-CHECK. This consists of five sturdy boards that make ten games of matching pictures, shapes, and colors. Each of the five boards is used both front and back; the ten sides have colorful and varied picture subjects: "Colors" and "More Colors," "Shapes" and "Shapes in Shapes," "Farm Animals," "Zoo Animals," "Fruits," "Vegetables," "Faces," and "Toys." A unique, patented feature of the boards is the self-checking device. The child moves a simple lever to reveal another pair of frames; when the two colors in these frames are the same, the pictures in the large frames have been matched correctly.

Scott, Foresman's latest set of boxed library materials, INVITATIONS TO STORY TIME, contains sixteen books selected just for preschool children: classic folk tales, exciting participation books, animal stories, selections for here and now, and the beloved "Mother Goose." In addition, colorful posters, storybook cut-outs and put-together puzzles of nursery rhyme characters are included to help disadvantaged children sense the richness they will someday find in books. Outstanding, too, are the two records of appropriate stories and poems read by Charlotte Huck.

WE READ PICTURES, available from Scott, Foresman, offers picture stories and picture exercise pages that give beginners practice in interpretation and perception skills they will need when they start to read.

The sixteen charts in SCIENCE IS WONDERING from Scott, Foresman are organized around four basic unit problems that have great appeal for the very young: "What Animals Make Good Pets?" "How Are Sounds Different?" "How Do We Use Wheels?" "How Are Plants Alike and Different?" In addition, there are available health and safety charts. Each of these sixteen charts aids the teacher in making important health and safety concepts meaningful for very young children.

One of the largest selections of preschool materials comes from Golden Press (8). These inexpensive books have been selected for preschool activities that help prepare the child for greater school success, assisting the teacher to meet such objectives as: strengthening the ability to listen purposefully and attentively; developing the ability to understand pictures; increasing manipulative skills and coordination; enlarging vocabulary; and developing acquaintance with and appreciation of books as a source of pleasure and information.

Some of these books include TOUCH AND FEEL ACTIVITY BOOKS in which children touch real wood, fabric, sandpaper; see themselves in a mirror; tip a seesaw to tell who is up and who is down.

Following are additional materials from Golden Press:

BLOCK BOOKS are shaped like building blocks with simple captions showing toys and other familiar objects.

PLAY AND LEARN BOOKS were designed especially to introduce young children to simple learning concepts, such as how to tie their shoes, how to tell time, how to count to ten.

PLAYBOOKS are fun books which help develop manipulative skills and the ability to relate pictures to the printed word.

GIANT STURDY BOOKS contain simple appealing stories with big clear pictures on every page for the youngest "readers" to enjoy.

GOLDEN SHAPE BOOKS have large type and big, uncluttered pictures to introduce many basic concepts.

The I CAN DO LIBRARY consists of three picture story books with learn-to-do activities which help the child to develop coordination of hand and eye and give him a sense of achievement. They are: "I Learn to Lace My Shoe," "I Learn to Button," and "I Learn to Tell Time."

The MERRIGOLD BOOKS contain a variety of enjoyable activities including coloring, cut-outs, puzzles, writing and counting exercises, and things to make.

PANORAMA BOOKS fold out so the children can see a parade of pictures, a free-standing panorama of twenty-two full-color panels with simple read-to-me text, which the child will soon learn to read for himself.

The widely known LITTLE GOLDEN BOOKS offer a variety of engrossing subjects in titles carefully selected for educational purposes. Many are about the young child's environment, giving him a sense of belonging. Others acquaint the child with the lives of people around him and extend his awareness of the world. Many are packed with information and behind the amusing stories of others is the serious purpose of helping the child prepare for adjustments.

LITTLE SILVER BOOKS are a special selection of LITTLE GOLDEN BOOKS which are long-time favorites of the preschooler.

Scholastic Magazines (23) publishes LET'S FIND OUT containing sensory-motor experiences, language development, and a healthy self-image for preschool children. For each child there are two four-page picture-magazines, one curriculum-related (full color), one news-related (black and white); there is also a story-supplement for school and home use. For the classroom, there are two 16½ by 22¼-in. posters (one in full color), two teaching guides, related multi-media samplings (such as a package of seeds or a package of gelatin for smelling and tasting), and a colorful delivery box, reusable for storage or projects. For the home of each child, there is a school-home supplement related to the month's learning, with a story or poem to be read aloud to the child at home. Also, notes to the parent are on each page of the picture-magazines.

THE EXPERIENTIAL DEVELOPMENT PROGRAM published by Benefic Press (3) is a program designed to provide the necessary developmental experience, or "readiness," a child needs to begin his formal learning. The two main areas of instruction are language arts and social studies. Therefore, the program is especially useful as an aid in developing oral communications skills and in building basic social concepts. However, the program does include some math, science, music and art.

THE EXPERIENTIAL DEVELOPMENT PROGRAM consists of three Teacher's "Big Books" with a pupil's independent "Activity Book" to accompany each. They are: "You and Your Family," "You and Your Friends," and "You and Others." The child-like printed illustrations allow any child, regardless of ethnic background, to identify with the subjects used in the illustrations. The uniqueness of the program is that it accommodates the child's stage of development and background experience. And because of the completeness of the programs, it is easy for both experienced and inexperienced teachers to orient themselves with it, and to teach it. Teachers who used the program during its testing period commented on the teaching ease and enjoyment derived from its use.

EXPERIENTIAL ENRICHMENT BOOKS, for use alone or with the EXPERIENTIAL DEVELOPMENT PROGRAM, are designed to help a child develop his self-identity and familiarize himself with his environment. They are useful as an aid in developing oral and reading readiness skills and in building social studies concepts. Also important, they develop an appreciation of the world of books.

Each of the four hardbound Enrichment Books contains thirty-two pages. They are arranged according to a unit and titled as follows: unit, "You and Your Family," individual titles, "I am Here," "My Family and I," "My Friends and I," and "I Can Do It."

The "STRUCTURAL READING SERIES, Book A," published by Singer (25) is a carefully organized, step-by-step program, making the child aware of the initial sounds of familiar words and how these sounds are represented by letters of the alphabet. The child begins to learn about the structural relationships of words and, thus, to understand, interpret, and enjoy what he reads.

Primary Playhouse (20) publishes many self-instructional materials useful for preschool children. All Primary Playhouse Flip-Its are preprogrammed, sequential, selective drills assigned in accordance to need. After the child has been taught the rudiments of initial sounding and the correct responses to the pictures, he can enjoy teaching himself with the Flip Its Initial Consonants. Also available are a set of twenty initial consonant charts coming in two colors with an attractive picture above and the initial letter below.

Many of the basic materials for preschool children are those that cannot be purchased: lots of space for movement, unhurried time, and many materials that they can use however they wish. Some of their favorite play materials may be cardboard boxes large enough for a child to climb in and out of, planks to walk on or perhaps raised in the center to form a seesaw, and rocks to climb on. All of these provide for child development. The child may enjoy small to large concentric circles taped or painted on the floor for use as paths or for jumping over, and they may prove to be an effective measure of the child's motor skills.

SELECTIVE BOOKS FOR PRESCHOOL CHILDREN
Alphabet Books

1. *ABC and Counting Book,* Phyllis Fraser, illus. Jack Sarkin (26)*

---

* Numbers in parentheses refer to Publisher Index.

2. *ABC Book,* illus. Dean Bryant (21)
3. *ABC Book,* illus. George and Doris Hauman (19)
4. *Alphabet Sampler, An,* illus. Zokeisha (4)
5. *Animal ABC,* illus. Garth Williams (8)
6. *Baby's First ABC, Words to Say* (19)
7. *Big Golden Animal ABC, The,* illus. Garth Williams (8)

Picture Books

1. *Baby Companion Books,* illus. Zokeisha (4)
2. *Baby Sees* (19)
3. *Baby's First Book,* illus. G. DeBeaulieu (19)
4. *Baby's First Book,* Garth Williams (8)
5. *Baby's First Counting Book* (19)
6. *Baby's Sturdi-Board Books* (26)
7. *Baby's Toys* (19)
8. *Child's First Picture Dictionary, A,* Lilian Moore (26)
9. *Great Big Animal Book,* illus. Rojanovsky (8)
10. *Great Big Car and Truck Book,* illus. Richard Scarry (8)
11. *Great Big Fire Engine Book,* illus. Tibor Gergely (8)
12. *Great Big Wild Animal Book,* illus. Feodor Rojankovsy (8)
13. *Little Red Hen, The,* Tony Palazzo, illus. by author (5)
14. *Living Story Books,* illus. Shiba (4)
15. *My Animal Friends* (19)
16. *My Baby Sister,* Patsy Scarry, illus. Sharon Koester (8)
17. *My Big Golden Counting Book,* Lilian Moore, illus. Garth Williams (8)
18. *My Counting Book,* Diane Sherman, illus. Sharon Koester (21)
19. *My First Book, What Baby Sees* (19)
20. *My First Toys* (19)
21. *Our Animal Friends,* illus. Wesley Dennis (19)
22. *Pets* (9)
23. *Throw a Kiss, Harry,* Mary Chalmers (10)
24. *Wonders of Nature,* Jane Werner Watson, illus. Eloise Wilkin (8)

Picture Story Books

1. *Benny and the Bear,* Barbee Oliver Carleton, illus. Dagmar Wilson (7)
2. *Big Book of the Real Circus, The,* Benjamin Brewster and Felix Sutton, illus. Gail Phillips and James Shucker (9)
3. *Big New School,* Evelyn Hastings, illus. Polly Jackson (7)
4. *Boy Who Would Not Say His Name,* Elizabeth Vreeken, illus. Leonard Shortall (7)

5. *Breman Town Musicians, The,* illus. Irma Wilde (21)
6. *Captain Kangaroo's Read-Aloud Book,* illus. Aurelius Battaglia (22)
7. *Choo Choo, the Little Switch Engine,* Wallack Wadsworth (21)
8. *Choo Choo Train,* Lillian Boyer Pennington, illus. Leonard Kessler (26)
9. *Cinderella,* Katharine Lee Bates, illus. Helen Endres and William Neebe (21)
10. *Cock, the Mouse, and the Little Red Hen, The,* illus. Helen Adler (21)
11. *Curious George Gets a Medal,* H. A. Rey (23)
12. *Elves and the Shoemaker, The,* illus. Manning De V. Lee (21)
13. *Enchanted Egg, The,* Peggy Burrows, illus. Elizabeth Webbe (21)
14. *Encyclopedia Britannica True-To-Life-Books* (6)
15. *Funny Hat, The,* Marjorie Barrows, illus. Dorothy Grider (21)
16. *Georgie's Pets,* Marion Conger, illus. Vera Neville (1)
17. *Goldilocks and the Three Bears,* illus. Tony Palazzo (5)
18. *Growing Up,* Jean Fritz, illus. Elizabeth Webbe (21)
19. *Helpful Henrietta,* Mabel Watts, illus. James Caraway (21)
20. *Hole in the Hill,* Marion Seyton, illus. Leonard Shortall (7)
21. *House That Jack Built, The,* illus. Anne Sellers Leaf (21)
22. *Jack and the Beanstalk,* illus. Anne Sellers Leaf (21)
23. *Johnny and the Birds,* Ian Munn, illus. Elizabeth Webbe (21)
24. *Jonny Goes to the Hospital,* Josephine Abbot Sever, illus. Mary Stevens (13)
25. *Jonathan and the Dragon,* Irwin Shapiro, illus. Tom Vroman (8)
26. *Just Follow Me,* Phoebe Erickson (7)
27. *Just Like Me,* Ruth Mackay, illus. Pelagie Doane (1)
28. *Little Bear Who Wanted Friends, The,* Edith Low, illus. Frances Eckhart (7)
29. *Little China Pig, The,* Dorothy Dickens Rawls, illus. Vivianne Blake (21)
30. *Little Crow, The,* Edith Osswald and Mary M. Reed, illus. Doris and Marion Henderson (11)
31. *Little Family, The,* Lois Lenski (5)
32. *Little Golden Library, The,* Mary Reed (8)
33. *Little Lamb's Hat,* Mary G. Phillips, illus. Eleanor Corwin (21)
34. *Little Lost Kitten,* Lois Levett, illus. Dale Maxey (22)
35. *Little Penguin,* Carrie Rarick, illus. Vivienne Blake DeMuth (21)
36. *Little Rabbit's Bath,* Miriam Clark Potter, illus. Vivienne Blake (21)
37. *Little Red Riding Hood,* illus. Anne Sellers Leaf (21)

38. *Once Upon a Time,* illus. Elizabeth Webbe (21)
39. *Pet for Peter,* A. J. Lilian Vandevere, illus. Adele Werber and Doris Laske (21)
40. *Peter Pat and the Policeman,* Catherine Stahlmann, illus. Dorothy Grider (21)
41. *Pony Engine, The,* Doris Garn, illus. Gregorio Prestopino (26)
42. *Read-Aloud Funny Stories,* Jane Thayer, illus. Crosby Newell (26)
43. *Read-Aloud Nursery Tales,* Caroline Kramer, illus. Phoebe Erickson (22)
44. *Rip Van Winkle,* Dorothy Bill Briggs, illus. Anne Sellers Leaf (21)
45. *Rumpelstilskin,* illus. Elizabeth Webbe (21)
46. *Scamper,* Marjorie Barrows, illus. Jean Tamburine (21)
47. *See the Circus,* H. A. Rey (13)
48. *Shadow the Cat,* Edith Osswald and Mary M. Reed, illus. Doris and Marion Henderson (11)
49. *Sleeping Beauty,* illus. Elizabeth Webbe (21)
50. *Sleepytime* (26)
51. *Snow White and the Seven Dwarfs,* Grimm, illus. Irma Wilde (21)
52. *Three Bears, The,* illus. Elizabeth Webbe (21)
53. *Three Little Ducks,* Rhoda Wyatt Woodstock, illus. Shusie (21)
54. *Tubby Turtle,* Helen Wing, illus. Helen Adler (21)
55. *Twilight Tales,* Marian Clark Potter, illus. Dean Bryant (21)
56. *Ugly Duckling, The,* Hans Christian Anderson, illus. Marge Opitz (21)

Verses

1. *Baby's First Mother Goose* (19)
2. *Child's Garden of Verses, A,* Robert Louis Stevenson, illus. Eve Garnett (18)
3. *Favorite Poems to Read Aloud,* illus. Art Kruz (26)
4. *Grandmas and Grandpas,* Alice Lour (22)
5. *Lenny's 20 Pennies,* Jean Conder Soule, illus. Ken Richards (17)
6. *Mother Goose Nursery Rhymes* (7)
7. *My Favorite Mother Goose Rhymes* (19)
8. *My Flower Book,* Dorothy Thompson Landis, illus. Elizabeth Webbe (21)
9. *Puffin Book of Verse, A,* Eleanor Graham, illus. Claudia Freedman (18)
10. *Rand McNally Elf Books* (21)
11. *Rand McNally Junior Elf Books* (21)

12. *Secret Place, The,* Dorothy Aldis, illus. Olivia H. Cole (23)
13. *Wynken, Blynken, and Nod and Other Nursery Rhymes,* Eugene Field, illus. Clare McKinley (21)
14. *Wynken, Blynken, and Nod,* Eugene Field, illus. Helen Page (7)

SELECTIVE BOOKS FOR TEACHERS OF PRESCHOOL CHILDREN

1. Burnett, D. K.: *Your Preschool Child: Making the Most of the Young from Two to Seven* (12)
2. Christianson, Helen; Rogers, Mary M.; and Ludlum, Blanche: *The Nursery School: Adventure in Living and Learning* (13)
3. Hefferman, H., and Todd, V. E.: *The Years Before School* (14)
4. Leavitt, J. E. (ed.): *Nursery-Kindergarten Education* (15)
5. Logan, Lillian: *Teaching the Young Child: Method of Preschool and Primary Education* (13)
6. Moore, Sally Beth, and Richards, Phyllis: *Teaching in the Nursery School* (10)
7. Pitcher, E. G., and Ames, L. B.: *The Guidance Nursery School* (10)
8. Rudolph, M.: *Living and Learning in the Nursery School* (10)

PUBLISHER INDEX

1. Abingdon Press, 201 8th Ave., S., Nashville 3, Tenn.
2. Allyn and Bacon, Inc., Rockleigh, N. J. 07647
3. Benefic Press, 1900 N. Narragansett Ave., Chicago, Ill. 60639
4. Crown Publishers, Inc., 419 Park Ave., S., New York, N. Y. 10016
5. Doubleday and Co., Inc., 575 Madison Ave., New York, N. Y. 10022
6. Encyclopedia Britannica Press, 425 N. Michigan Ave., Chicago, Ill. 60611
7. Follett Publishing Co., 1010 W. Washington Blvd., Chicago, Ill. 60607
8. Golden Press, Inc., 850 3rd Ave., New York, N. Y. 10022
9. Grosset and Dunlap, Inc., 1107 Broadway, New York, N. Y. 10010
10. Harper and Row, Publishers, Inc., 49 E. 33rd St., New York, N. Y. 10016
11. Heath and Co., D. C., 285 Columbus Ave., Boston 16, Mass.
12. Holt, Rinehart and Winston, 383 Madison Ave., New York, N. Y.
13. Houghton Mifflin Co., 2 Park St., Boston 7, Mass.
14. Macmillan Co., 60 5th Ave., New York, N. Y. 10011
15. McGraw-Hill Book Co., 330 W. 42nd St., New York, N. Y.
16. Milton Bradley Co., 74 Park St., Springfield, Mass. 01101
17. Parents' Magazine Press, Inc., 52 Vanderbilt Ave., New York, N. Y. 10017

18. Penguin Books, Inc., 3300 Clipper Mill Rd., Baltimore 11, Md.
19. Platt and Munk Co., Inc., 200 5th Ave., New York, N. Y. 10010
20. Primary Playhouse, Sherwood, Oregon
21. Rand McNally and Co., P. O. Box 7600, Chicago, Ill. 60680
22. Random House, Inc., 457 Madison Ave., New York, N. Y. 10022
23. Scholastic Magazines, Inc., 902 Sylvan Ave., Englewood Cliffs, N. J.
24. Scott, Foresman and Co., 433 E. Erie St., Chicago, Ill. 60611
25. Singer Co., Inc., L. W., 249 N. Erie Blvd., Syracuse 2, N. Y.
26. Wonder Books, 1107 Broadway, New York, N. Y. 10010

Chapter 11

CHILDREN WITH VISUAL DISABILITIES

JEANETTE BURKE

Many children who have a complete or partial loss of vision can and do attend their neighborhood public schools with assistance provided through an itinerant teacher program. They are completely integrated with sighted children. For these children a preschool program is of paramount importance and should be considered as a necessary part of their education.

The purpose of the itinerant program is that children who have partial vision or who are totally blind can remain in a regular public school rather than live away from home at a school for the blind. Through the itinerant program they will attend school with sighted children from kindergarten through high school. Why not also encourage them to attend a preschool program with sighted children?

Administrators of special educational programs for children with visual disabilities should consider beginning their itinerant programs at the preschool level, rather than the kindergarten level. The children with a vision problem should be included in a preschool program with sighted children. Such a program would be most successful if an itinerant teacher-consultant is involved.

Presently, in most itinerant programs the child who has a vision disability is expected to enter kindergarten with sighted children. The child is handicapped not because of his limited vision but because he has not been adequately prepared.

Children with vision disabilities develop in essentially the same way as seeing children, but usually slower. Because of this, the tendency has been to wait a year longer before placement in a kindergarten program, or to keep them in kindergarten for more than one year until they are "ready" for first grade. However, these children need more than an extra year in which to mature. They need experiences and special instruction. At the same time, they need close association with seeing children.

A child with a vision loss needs the same experiences as a seeing child but he also needs exposure to many areas that are normally taken for granted. Concrete objects must be brought to the child so he knows what they look like. The young child who cannot see may talk about a coffee pot but unless he has actually felt one he does not know what it looks like. He may picture it entirely different from the way it looks. A child with partial vision may know what a leaf is but he may not know that leaves are at the tops of trees because he can't see that far. There are many things this child must learn that the seeing child knows just by seeing.

The child who cannot see needs concrete experiences as well as verbal approaches. What other children learn by imitation this child must learn through physical contact. We know this but yet we allow many of these children to begin kindergarten without any notion of what the simplest objects look like. Then we expect them to begin developing concept formations. Additionally, the child should be provided with insight into experiences and objects at the same time as children with sight. They should not be halfway through high school before they "see" what an airplane looks like. A verbal description alone is not giving them enough. A verbal description alone cannot convey an appreciation of massiveness and detail.

Many children with low vision have been mainly given verbal descriptions and have consequently developed language problems. Parents have sometimes anticipated the child's needs to such an extent that his speech development is delayed through a lack of need. Conversely, many children tend to constantly verbalize as a means of self amusement since visual stimulation is lacking. In either case a preschool program would discourage rambling verbalization in the classroom as well as stimulate vocabulary growth.

Another reason for preschool preparation is that upon entering kindergarten a child is expected to be prepared in certain areas and ready to learn. Several years ago kindergarten would not have been so demanding. However, kindergarten curriculums have been expanded to such an extent that much more is now expected. More emphasis is now being placed on reading readiness skills and concept formation than ever before. Children in kindergarten do much more than play. They are instructed in language development, number concepts, and social institutions.

Reading readiness is now a large part of the primary education program. For instance, similarities and differences of objects are distinguished in preparation for later distinguishing letters in the alphabet. How can a child who has never seen or felt an object be expected to know the differences involved? These activities are used as a prelude to print reading, but these kinds of distinctions should also be made for a much longer period, and with greater frequency for the child who is going to be a braille reader. Braille reading requires much finer distinctions. If a child is going to be a braille reader he should be prepared for this before entering kindergarten.

A child with a vision loss is perhaps most behind in social experiences. This could be his "primary handicap" rather than his limited vision or loss of sight particularly because he is unaware of social dynamics and expectations. In many cases kindergarten is the first experience away from home. Often it is the first time the child ever has been expected to play with other children.

The child who cannot see is not attracted to the toy that another child is playing with, and is therefore not tempted to join him in play. Often he will only play with things placed in his hands. This child must be *taught* how to play. Playing is so natural to most children that it is difficult to realize that it must be taught to sightless children. Often these children do not notice other children. Because of this it is important to provide a setting where they will be exposed to other children.

Mention should be made of preschool programs that are entirely for children with visual disabilities. Although such programs would be geared to their needs they would be associating only with other children who have vision disabilities. A child should adjust to the seeing world and attend school with normal children. If, in the preschool program, the child with a vision problem is with normal children but receives the services and help of a teacher-consultant, he would still acquire the basic skills he needs to function in kindergarten. At the same time, he will have the advantages of associating with normal children. Experience has shown that children who associate with normal children are more nearly normal themselves.

Often a very young child does not realize he has a vision problem. Many children who have little vision think that all people see the way they do. Very young totally blind children hear the word "blind" but do not comprehend its meaning or attach any stigma to it. Their self image is not one of a "handicapped" person. If they are included in a preschool program they will develop self esteem in knowing that they can do what other children can do. They will learn that there are many kinds of activities in which they can participate.

These children must develop a wholesome self concept by knowing that they can do what other children do before they learn that they cannot do some things that other children can do.

Without adequate preparation for a kindergarten class the child with a vision problem may experience feelings of failure that could have been prevented. Self-confidence is such an important factor in learning that it should be guarded and developed. Irreparable damage can be done if a child expects failure because he has become accustomed to it.

A major goal in educating a child with a vision disability as with any child is to enable him to be independent. It should also be a goal to enable him to be independent at as early an age as possible.

How much more self-esteem a child would have if he did not have to ask for help to do such simple tasks as zipping his jacket or buttoning his shirt. All too frequently a child who cannot see is well through grammar school (if not high school) before he can tie his own shoes. The need for help in these everyday skills handicaps him more than his lack of sight. The inability to perform everyday tasks is not because of a vision disability but because he has not been instructed in these areas.

One should not necessarily expect a child of three years to have the coordination necessary to tie his shoes—a child with good sight has a problem at that age. However, the child who cannot see should be given training that will prepare him for this type of skill. Stringing beads, for instance, is a readiness skill for tying shoes. Frames, such as those devised by Montessori, are especially helpful in preparation for buttoning clothes.

These types of skills are explained at the preschool level. By kindergarten, children are expected to know how to dress and care for themselves. It is true that the child who cannot see would need more instruction in these areas than the average child, but the instruction could be done by the teacher-consultant who is working along with the preschool teacher.

What is especially needed are materials that would be helpful in the area of daily living skills. At the present time there are no curriculum guides or structured outlines concerning the teaching of daily living skills to children with visual disabilities, which magnifies problems in educational programming.

Another area where independence is of prime importance is mobility. Mobility training should begin early enough so that with some instruction a child would be able to walk from the school bus to his room, around his classroom and to the cafeteria. Kindergarten should not be his first experience with mobility training. At the preschool level he should have been made aware of the availability of sound clues and various mobility suggestions.

How can a child learn social skills, independent behavior, and daily living skills in a kindergarten program where he is expected to play and do work at the level of other children his age? It is frustrating to attempt all of this in one kindergarten year. How can a teacher-consultant be expected to keep the child who has little or no sight at the same level with the other children if he has never played with another child, never seen a farm animal or has not been allowed to put on his own clothes?

The itinerant program places a further handicap on the child by expecting him to compete with sighted children at an early age without preparation. This is not to say that he should not compete with sighted children, but only that he should be prepared. Many of these children do not ordinarily compete without encouragement and have a low competitive spirit. Telling a child that other children can count to ten may not arouse his interest in learning to count to ten. This is part of a learning orientation that can be developed in a preschool program. Listening skills, the ability to follow directions, and verbal expression are some of the areas that facilitate learning. Lack of these skills aften slows the rate of learning.

The child who will receive assistance through an itinerant program must have a proper learning orientation. He must also be even more independent than the child at a residential school for the blind because of the necessity to perform at the same level as sighted children in the same grade.

Parents seem to get as much out of a preschool program as their children. Many times the parents of a child with a visual disability are in need of as much counseling and instruction as the child himself as noted in Chapter 2. It would be most helpful if this guidance could begin well before school age.

Overprotection is a common problem among parents who have children who cannot see. They are so concerned over the possible dangers that may befall their children that they do not allow them to play normally. Many of these children have never been allowed to climb a tree or to run down a hill. In a preschool program they would be allowed and encouraged to participate in physical activity.

Parents will be able to observe their child doing things they would never have permitted. Parents may hold their breath when they see the child climb a jungle gym with the other children, but they will slowly come to realize that their child can play, and that perhaps they should allow him to go on the playground like other children. Concurrently, the child is learning what his capabilities are in regard to physical activity. The parent and the child will be able to set more realistic limitations.

Parents are often at a loss in deciding what type of educational program is best for their child. They are aware that they could send their child to a school for the blind, but many times are not aware of an itinerant program. Even if they are aware of an itinerant program in their area they usually do not fully understand the services provided. They wonder if perhaps they are doing their child an injustice if they do not send him to a school specifically designed for children who cannot see. They are uncertain whether their child would succeed in a school with sighted children. They are also anxious about the attitudes of the sighted children toward their child.

A preschool program would present the parents with an opportunity to see their child in a normal school setting. They would be able to observe their child playing with other children and notice how accepting young children are.

Another benefit for the parents would be to become aware of the child's needs and learn about his weaknesses. They may be surprised to discover that the vision problem is not as much a limitation as the observation that the child does not yet relate to other children. Assuming proper communication exists in the program, the parent can assist in solving many problems at home.

The teacher-consultant also would benefit from working with the child at the preschool level. She could consult more effectively with the classroom kindergarten teacher if she were already familiar with the youngster. She could advise more realistically and assure the teacher of the child's capabilities. She would be aware of the child's needs and could concentrate on helping the child learn along with the other children. If the teacher-consultant meets the child for the first time at the beginning of kindergarten, it takes many weeks to get to know the child's potential as well as hours of instruction to develop necessary skills.

School principals are sometimes reluctant about enrolling a child with a vision problem. There is frequently a difference of opinion regarding the itinerant program. Many school principals assume that such a child should, without question, be sent to a school for the blind. The typical solution is that they will agree to have the child in a class with normal children strictly on a "trial" basis. The teacher-consultant could use the preschool program as evidence of preparation. The success of the child in a preschool program may convince the administrators of the feasibility of a child with a vision loss attending school with normal youngsters.

CASE STUDY

Name: Marcia D.
Age: five years
Medical diagnosis of visual defect: optic atrophy

At birth Marcia appeared to be a normal, healthy baby. Medical examinations at one year revealed a brain tumor which resulted in optic atrophy and partial paralysis of the right limbs. Surgery was performed to remove the tumor, and little, if any, useful vision remained.

Marcia appeared to be of normal intelligence although no tests had been administered. Her speech was good with poor language development. She was an active, alert child who seemed to be very happy.

Marcia attended a nursery school at the local Association for the Blind for approximately two months. Due to its discontinuation, Marcia could not remain in the program for the following school year. The director of the program noted that Marcia showed some improvement in the short time she attended, particularly in the area of daily living skills.

Apparently, several professional people had recommended placing Marcia at the School for the Blind. However, since Mrs. D. wanted Marcia to remain at home she desired educational services in a regular school. She was referred by the Association to an itinerant program.

At the time of referral Marcia was five years of age and had just been enrolled in a neighborhood kindergarten class with sighted children.

Mr. and Mrs. D. experienced considerable anxiety over Marcia, caused by extensive medical examinations, surgery and the resulting disabilities. There appeared to be dissention between the parents as to realistic expectations and educational experiences for Marcia. Guilt feelings over the disabilities were evident. The parents exhibited an extreme desire for normality, reflecting a lack of acceptance toward her disabilities. Every attempt they made at normality negated progress in this direction. They created many inhibitions in the child. They did not want to admit to her blindness and in hoping for any remaining vision, discouraged any attempt Marcia made to touch things. In fearing public reaction to Marcia's disability, they sheltered her so much that she was not taken out of the home very often.

It was immediately apparent when observing Marcia that she did not touch things in order to see what they were. She would continually guess at the name of an object. She expressed her feeling that it is wrong to touch things. As she entered kindergarten she had very little conception about how most objects look. She could verbalize about an object but had no image in her mind. She was unaware of the most simple things including those common items in her own home.

Marcia had also had very little contact with other children. Her brother was just an infant and she was not encouraged to play with the neighborhood children. At the time she began kindergarten, she would only play by herself. She would go off alone and become very angry if a child came near her or her toys. It was only after several weeks in school that she would allow a child to play next to her.

Marcia would constantly verbalize in class and could not readily participate in group activities. She was not functioning at the same level as most other children in the kindergarten.

Marcia should have attended a preschool program with sighted children for an entire year. The teacher-consultant would have worked with her for a year before she entered kindergarten and would have been aware of her needs. She would have provided a year of instruction to prepare Marcia for kindergarten.

The parents would have become acquainted much sooner with the itinerant program and would have become familiar with the services provided. They would have realized the educational alternatives between the itinerant program and the program offered at the School for the Blind. Counseling with the parents could have commenced at an earlier date eliminating many disagreements between them regarding educational placement and proper treatment of their child. They would have been encouraged to accept responsibility in providing meaningful experiences for Marcia. They would have observed Marcia playing with other children and have realized the need for more social and physical contact with peers. A preschool program could have prepared Marcia socially for kindergarten play activities.

If the teacher-consultant was involved with Marcia in a preschool program, the initial contact with the school administrator would have been made by her rather than by the parents. Considering the fact that the administrator did not approve of Marcia's enrollment in a normal school, many problems would have been eliminated by having first discussed them with the teacher-consultant.

Most children with visual disabilities need instruction about objects that normal children automatically recognize. How much more instruction did Marcia need since she had never felt things? Many field trips had to be made to familiarize her with the world around her so that later her reading experiences would be meaningful. Concrete objects had to be presented until she learned that she could see with her hands.

The paralysis of her right hand necessitated the development of tactile responses in her left hand. She was encouraged to use her left hand as much as possible since two hands are required to read braille. A therapist was contacted to provide whatever therapy may increase the strength in the affected limb. A brace on her right leg needed frequent replacement to accommodate her growth.

It would be impossible to teach Marcia the many concepts she lacked at the same time as teaching her all the subject matter she was expected to learn in kindergarten. Consequently, she will probably have to repeat kindergarten in order to achieve the level of readiness appropriate for entering first grade. How much better would her first experience in school have been if she had been ready—if she had the social competencies, the independent actions and the concepts a child usually possesses upon entering kindergarten.

Chapter 12

CHILDREN WITH HEARING DISABILITIES

BETH CHAPMAN RINGQUIST*

INTRODUCTION

A SEARCH OF professional literature has revealed a paucity of information concerning programs for hearing-impaired infants, those under the age of three years. Wooden (1962) reports that "A few days schools initiate programs for infants as young as one year of age." Grammatico (1964) wrote that "Education of the preschool deaf child is a relatively new addition to the education of deaf children in the United States; however, the number of programs is increasing yearly." An interesting note is provided by Calvert and Baltzer (1967) when they state that ". . . very few people are being trained specifically to work with preschool-age hearing-impaired children in any way." And, Luterman (1967) commented that ". . . formal programs for the child with a hearing impairment rarely begin before age three."

The belief that the hearing-impaired child should not have to wait until age five or six before his education commences is stated succinctly by Harris (1964): "The education of all children begins from the moment of birth, not in kindergarten or first grade. The deaf child's education should not be delayed either. . . . If you start training your child while he is very young, he is at a stage of development where doing things over and over again is enjoyable." Lady Ewing (1963) concurs with Harris, with the statement that "Beginning of training before the age of eighteen months can help much to avoid a common risk that a deaf child may become domineering or uncooperative."

The first four authorities cited above emphasize that programs for

---

*Thanks to Mr. Douglas K. Hinton for his assistance as supervisor of the project reported on in this chapter.

the hearing-impaired child under the age of three are not numerous. There are not many people trained specifically to teach this age group, either.

Programs that are currently available for the age group under three are so few that some of them can be mentioned here. Griffiths (1964) wrote about the HEAR Foundation program for hearing-handicapped children under three years of age. The youngest infant in this program was one month old. A program in Manchester University, England, was reported by Lady Ewing (1964). This program, part of a research project to determine conditions in which very young children can be given effective training in their homes, was directed especially to children with hearing losses who are under the age of two years. Parent guidance was stressed in another program reported by Simmons (1966), where infants were enrolled as early as eighteen months. Calvert and Baltzer (1967) have described a home management program for hearing preschoolers (ranging from twenty-four months to five years) within the framework of a comprehensive preschool program. Horton (1968) has described a program designed for parents of hearing-impaired children aged seven months to three years that emphasizes demonstration of procedures to be employed within the home.

THE STUDY

A recent survey (Chapman, 1968) was conducted from the Speech and Hearing Center at the State University College at Fredonia, New York, to find out what kinds of programs are available for hearing-impaired infants (from birth to three years of age). A questionnaire was devised to determine how many programs were currently existing and to gain information about them. The questionnaire was mailed to 126 randomly selected schools for the deaf located in the United States and Canada. Of the 72 questionnaires returned (before data were compiled) only eighteen had programs for infants. Six other schools were planning, or had initiated, home training or short summer sessions involving parents of this age group.

The newest program had been in existence for only six months. The majority of the programs were either tutorial or a combination of day school-tutorial. There was only one residential school for this age group. Referrals to these programs came most frequently from (1) pediatricians; (2) speech and hearing diagnostic centers, and (3) parents. Techniques for amplification of sound within the educational settings was quite similar. All students wore body aides. Group trainers and/or induction loop amplification also were utilized. Audiologists, teachers certified to teach deaf and/or hearing-impaired children, and psychologists were employed by most of the schools. The primary method of instruction was orally oriented. Parental involvement in all of these centers was very highly emphasized. With children this young, parental cooperation was felt necessary in order to achieve goals. Information concerning curriculum was available from only six of the eighteen programs.

As another aspect of the study, questionnaires were sent to parents of all children who were enrolled in "communication skills" classes at the Fredonia clinic, to find out what questions these parents have concerning home management and training of their children.

The age at which parents first suspected a hearing impairment ranged from one month to six and one-half years. Factors causing most suspicion of such a loss were: (1) failure to develop normal speech and language patterns; and (2) failure to respond to speech and/or loud noises. Over half of these families consulted their family doctor first about their suspicions of hearing impairment. Referrals to the Fredonia center were made by several different agencies and professional persons. The highest number were referred by another hearing and speech diagnostic center. The length of time between diagnosis of hearing loss and acquirement of hearing aid varied from six months to two years; however, the mean time period was approximately one year.

Questions from the parents were highly individual for the most part; however, they can be grouped into four broad categories: (1) education; (2) behavior of the child; (3) community relations; and (4) vocational prospects. Over 70 percent of those questioned had no knowledge of hearing loss in children before their child's impairment was diagnosed. The most prevalent and reportedly effective method of discipline was the "old-fashioned" spanking. This did not differ much from discipline found to be most effective with other siblings in the families. Fifty percent of those reporting made no alteration in their handling of their child after learning of his hearing impairment, except in the area of education. Most parents felt that there was a normal sibling relationship within the home. Seventy-five percent noted a change in behavior after the child had worn his hearing aid.

This second part of the total survey would have more validity with a larger population (only twelve of twenty-four questionnaires were returned); however, it was designed for a select group of persons.

CONCLUSIONS

From the results of the questionnaire designed for administrators and/or supervisors, it appears that there are very few infant programs available in schools for the deaf randomly selected from a directory of schools for the deaf in the United States and Canada. There were only eighteen programs available from the seventy-two replies. The majority of these eighteen schools have established their programs for infants in such a manner that they are definitely dependent upon parental involvement and cooperation. Most of these schools stated that they teach the parent rather than the child.

There were several comments on the questionnaires returned from the schools which were impossible to tabulate. One Canadian school described its program as consisting of home visitation with two full-time teachers traveling continuously throughout northern and eastern Ontario to provide parent guidance. Visits occur either once each week or once each month (depending upon geographical location of the home) from the time the child is referred until he is ready for school. One school mentioned that it has provision for children with or without severe hearing impairment who present a severe language disorder. Only children with severe hearing losses were reported as being enrolled in another school. Two schools commented that they had one and two children, respectively, enrolled in their infant programs. An overwhelming majority of those making comments emphasized the role of parents in their programs. Another school administrator stressed that although his school utilized any method to get the child personally involved, this was all planned in advance, a contradictory explanation.

It appeared, from these comments, that the individuals responsible for answering the questionnaire were greatly interested in their programs. The willingness to share information concerning curriculums, together with invitations to visit and observe, was amazing. There seemed to be little possessiveness, or unwillingness to share whatever information was available. For example, the administrator of one school wished the survey "Good Luck;" another was kind enough to suggest references for review of the literature. The administrator of another school took time to write, stating that since his school had no infant program, he was forwarding the questionnaire to another school.

The answers given by parents on their questionnaires reflect their primary concerns. Their questions concerning their hearing-impaired children imply a need for much more involvement and counseling. Would parents of children enrolled in the schools reporting have had similar questions? Because 75 percent of the parents answering acknowledged lack of information concerning hearing impairment in children, it is evident that the heavy emphasis upon the involvement of parents in different schools is not misplaced.

DISCUSSION

These two surveys can be considered to be only an initial phase in this area of specialized education. Possibilities for future research on such programs and parental involvement appear to be unlimited. A longitudinal study would provide data regarding any change of procedures or emphasis from that currently presented by parents and administrators of hearing-impaired children. Such a study would indicate modification of trends in identification, referral and habilitative procedures. This survey is only an initial step towards research in this area.

The preceding pages of this chapter have been presented to demonstrate how very little is being done in the United States and in Canada for the very young child with a hearing loss. The first three years of life are very important to every individual. These years should not be ignored when a child has been diagnosed as having a hearing loss. The John Tracy Clinic Correspondence Course* is available; while it is an excellent course for the parents, it should be a secondary source of help. Providing counsel and suggestions by mail is difficult. It is

---

*See end of chapter.

hoped that eventually enough educators will be available so this course will become supplementary material rather than the only source to which some parents have to turn for help.

MATERIALS FOR PARENTS

Book: *If You Have A Deaf Child.* Urbana, University of Illinois Press, 1965.

Correspondence: The John Tracy Clinic Correspondence Course, 924 West 37th Street, Los Angeles, California.

Magazine: *The Volta Review.* Published by the Volta Bureau, 1537 Thirty-Seventh Street, N. W., Washington 7, D. C. (monthly).

Workbook: *What's Its Name? A Guide to Speech and Hearing Development,* by Jean Utley. Urbana, University of Illinois Press, 1968.

REFERENCES

1. Calvert, D. R. and Baltzer, Susanna: Home management in a comprehensive preschool program for hearing impaired children. *Exceptional Children,* 253, December, 1967.
2. Chapman, Beth: Unpublished research paper for completion of Master's Degree. S. U. C., Fredonia, New York, 1968.
3. Connor, Leo: Research in education of the deaf in the United States. *Volta Rev., 65,*523, November, 1963.
4. Ewing, Lady E. C.: Some psychological variables in the training of young deaf children. *Volta Rev., 65,*68, February, 1963.
5. Grammatico, Leahea: Building a language foundation at the preschool level. *Volta Rev., 66,*378, September, 1964.
6. Griffiths, Ciwa: The auditory approach for preschool deaf children. *Volta Rev., 66,*387, September, 1964.
7. Harris, Grace M.: For parents of very young deaf children. *Volta Rev., 66,*19, January, 1964.
8. Horton, Kathryn: Home demonstration teaching for parents of very young deaf children. *Volta Rev., 70,*97, February, 1968.
9. Luterman, David M.: A parent-oriented nursery program for preschool deaf children. *Volta Rev., 69,*515, October, 1967.
10. Simmons, Audrey A.: Language growth for the prenursery deaf child. *Volta Rev., 68,*201, March, 1966.
11. Wooden, Harley: Dramatized language for the deaf. *Exceptional Children, 29,*155, December, 1962.

Chapter 13

A PARENT'S VIEW OF PRESCHOOL PROGRAMS

MARY LANG AND JOAN COBB

IN THE PRECEDING PAGES you have read of the most recent developments in educational help for preschool children with learning difficulties.

The inception and continued existence of this and all types of programs for children with learning and behavior problems will depend largely on parents' understanding and function and importance of such a program.

Due to the lack of knowledge and understanding of learning problems in all professions, in their search for help parents find communication continually breaking down. This leads to inaction, confusion and resentment on the part of everyone concerned. Parents feel themselves facing a series of brick walls with no solutions in sight.

While medical and educational people will sympathize with parents, each feels it is the other's responsibility to provide help for the child. Help when given too often is superficial. Professionals seem unaware that by paying only lip-service to this problem they inadvertently seal the doom of these children, at least as perceived by parents.

What is heartbreaking for many parents is the glaring fact that with proper help at an early age many children with problems could have been productive citizens contributing to society. Even more heartbreaking is the terrible realization that many professionals having contact with these children do not even see their potential, but take the attitude that this end result was inevitable. Parents' feelings of desperation and anger are justified when they must stand by and watch their children's future slowly fade for lack of proper help.

When no help is found, the situation within home and school can become critical. The situation at home is compounded by pride ("We are intelligent, well-behaved parents, so our children must follow suit") or guilt ("What am I doing wrong in bringing up my child?") Husband and wife are apt to blame each other, bringing on family strife that aggravates the original problem. The situation at school is compounded by conventional classroom curriculum and procedures.

Parents should not blame themselves for having a child who will not conform in either learning or behavior. It is not your fault. It is your fault if you do not assume the responsibility of finding out what the child needs and then fighting until those needs are met. Wrapping yourselves in a cocoon of confusion and apathy is done at the expense of the child's future.

HOW PARENTS CAN EFFECT CHANGE

Step 1

In dealing with a search for help, parents are asking two basic questions: "What is the matter with my child," and "What can I do to help him?"

We recommend strongly your affiliation with a local parent group. The name of this group may vary depending on location.*

For information about local chapters of the Association for Children with Learning Disabilities (ACLD) write to International ACLD.* The international ACLD is a well established, nonprofit organization whose purpose is to advance the education and general well-being of children with normal, potentially normal, or above-average intelligence who have learning disabilities arising from perceptual, conceptual or subtle coordinative problems, sometimes accompanied by behavior difficulties.

While all parents' organizations may not be effective, many are extremely persuasive and will benefit from active support. Many educational programs for children did not begin until parents demanded action. A large group of parents is helpful; however, in many instances as many as twenty are able to bring about needed change. Once part of an organized group, it is a good idea to become as knowledgeable in the area of learning problems in children as possible. There are many sources of information, available in the form of books,

---

* See resource list at the end of this chapter.

films, conferences, newsletters, publication and journals (see the resource list).

It can now become your job to educate your school system and community. There is little point in arguing for your child's education until you yourself are aware of what is needed. Schools have for a long time oversimplified your child's problems and adopted the attitude of waiting. It is easy to procrastinate and see how things will be next year. Parents hesitate to question a school's expertise. After all, education is their job and for too long parents have not been encouraged to become involved. This attitude on the part of parents is indeed in need of change. Whose children are they? No one is as vitally concerned as you about this person, and in the final analysis no one but you is responsible for his well being. Many knowledgeable ACLD parents find themselves in the ludicrous position of knowing more than the professionals. This situation will exist until professionals accept their responsibility to these children.

Step 2

Assuming you have some evaluation of your child's difficulty you may begin to work toward a proper program for him.

Meet with your school principal and see what is offered to meet the needs of your child. Always follow the proper channels of authority. You will find many schools will have some kind of program for slow learners or underachievers. If these are offered, look into the situation carefully. These may prove to be a dumping ground for the many children who are not achieving. Rarely are these children evaluated, nor are individual programs devised. The program can consist of a watered-down curriculum using identical methods of presentation that have already failed. The parents, possessing knowledge of multisensory teaching approaches, and realizing that no two children's difficulties are the same, that methods and materials must differ according to needs, will spot these attempts at remediation.

Often classes in remediation, such as speech and reading, are not entirely helpful due to their limited approach. The remedial teacher will attempt to reinforce the work in the one approach to reading currently used in that school system. In other words, if your school is curriculum-oriented rather than child-oriented you will need to be prepared for action. Even though children are allowed to progress at their own pace, no other approach is ever used for those who can't learn.

Step 3

The next step should be a meeting with such school personnel as the teachers, principal, psychologist and school superintendent. At this meeting you must present all known information about your child and the many other children with similar needs. Take a small amount of basic literature with you. No matter what the results seem to be, don't give up, don't get hysterical, but be convinced you are right in pursuing your cause. Let them know you intend to persist.

Step 4

Support your stand by enlisting the aid of several members of your board of education. It is time-consuming but helpful if you are first able to approach them separately rather than in a group. Again take good but brief literature with you.

After you have explained the need to the school and to the members of the school board, have some concrete suggestions for their review. These will differ depending on your locality and school structure. Make the first demands reasonable and build from there.

Step 5

If you have followed these procedures and received no satisfaction, we suggest you contact your state commissioner of education. For children with learning and behavior problems to receive maximum help, legislation and funding is still needed in many states.

Assuming your school has agreed to start a program for these children and your child is receiving help, there will remain an urgent need to expand and improve these efforts. Your continued interest and support is necessary for proper education, preschool through twelfth grade. Never assume this will be automatic.

TO THE PROFESSIONAL

Parents are certainly not the only ones beset with a child's problems.

There also are the professionals. The medical, neurological, psychological, and educational areas all become involved.

The comment most commonly made by the medical profession is, "Don't worry, he will out grow it." In our present-day society, this does not hold true, especially with the accelerated demands placed on school children. At best the child learns to compensate, but in doing so he develops emotional problems that far outweigh the original disability.

A neurological examination may or may not be indicated. The important thing to keep in mind is that the EEG (electroencephlogram) can seem to be normal. This does not necessarily mean there is no learning problem.

Psychological testing may begin to pinpoint areas of difficulty, and educational testing should give further insight into difficulties. Then there must be specific prescriptive suggestions for remediation at home and school. Remediation begun at an early age will insure the greatest success for the child.

How can professionals help us?

As parents in our association with professional people, we have become aware of the terrible complacency and confusion that exists within schools and communities concerning problem children. The American Dream—the pursuit of excellence—of pushing all children into a narrow pattern of achievement and behavior is tolerable, but only if the child has the inherent ability to measure up. When they do not we are apt to look down our noses and say, "He could do better if he tried." It does not occur to us that many children have tried and failed over and over, that they need your help. Children are not born failures. They do not enter this world planning to have poor behavior or to fail in math or reading. They want very much to fit and be accepted by both adults and peers. Thus society makes its own failures when these attitudes exist.

While many professionals, both medical and educational, will sympathize with parents and the needs of the child, each feels it is the other's responsibility. There is a definite lack of ability to communicate in the different professional disciplines, and parents and children are passed back and forth between the many professional groups with no one offering constructive help.

There are many children with a large variety of problems, and subsequent needs; therefore, a variety of reactions and concerns may be expressed by parents. One child who will be of utmost concern to the parents at an early age is one who is usually hyperactive. By the time this child reaches the age of three or four parents become anxious and distraught when they realize that at the magic age of five he must enter kindergarten and conform to standards set by society. Up to this point the child has been a constant source of upheaval within the family. Suddenly he will leave the safe protection of the home and others will be looking at him. The parent feels that the child's actions are a reflection on his upbringing and environment.

Adults who come in contact with this child may have an archaic attitude and strengthen this hypothesis. Parents are confused, defensive, and guilty. Before the child enters kindergarten, the parents may seek help from various professionals and may receive little or no assistance. Someone along the route may suggest medication which may or may not help and indicate that the child may have some difficulty in school. This the parents suspected in the first place. Some may even define the area of difficulty but be unable to offer constructive suggestions. They expect this from the schools. The child's records go with him to school but too often are put to no positive use. School personnel are often unable to decipher the reports because of their lack of comprehension involving the total area of learning problems in children. Teachers with some understanding are unable to structure positive programs because of the absence of total commitment and support on the part of the administration.

As the child enters kindergarten his performance is poor and he begins his long road to failure. This is carried over in his relationship with the home and the community.

Other children to be considered are those who do not overtly disturb anyone at home, but sit quietly and patiently doing very little. These children also enter kindergarten, their performance is poor and they proceed through each year quietly failing. Parents are often lulled into false security by school personnel and are told that junior will blossom forth soon. This is what is known in school circles as the "late bloomer." We know of some "late bloomers" who have reached their teens and are still waiting for spring. These children then become known as the "underachievers" and "slow learners."

Had these children had the help of an adequate preschool program such as is described in the preceeding chapters, with on-going follow-up assistance in subsequent grades, much of the confusion, fear and frustration on the part of the parents and the child would have been alleviated.

Some school districts are becoming increasingly aware of the urgency and need that exists. Some are even trying to do something about it. A few are having limited success. Others are groping in confusion.

SUGGESTED GOALS FOR SCHOOLS

Action on the part of schools is long overdue. Following are some observations and some suggestions for action:

Our colleges should be involved in preparing regular classroom teachers for working with children who have problems in learning and behavior.

In some states colleges do not even require elementary teachers to complete a course in how to teach reading as part of their certification.

Reading specialists or remedial reading teachers are often regular classroom teachers who have completed one or two courses in reading instruction. This is hardly sufficient when you consider the diversity of our children's problems and the varied methods needed to evaluate and work with them in the area of reading. Reading specialists often use the same method of reading instruction the child has failed in for several years, never considering or indeed recognizing that the method or approach used will not work with this particular child.

Physical education teachers leave our colleges ready to teach physical fitness with no awareness of the developmental process of growth and its relationship to academic success.

Speech therapists are concerned more with articulation than developmental language.

Classroom teachers quickly establish their method of teaching. If the child does not respond, it is somehow HIS problem. They rarely consider the need for different methods and materials. Teachers know nothing of the necessary prerequisites to learning that pave the way to successful scholastic progress.

Until our colleges recognize and adjust their archaic teacher preparation courses, there is no alternative but for schools to assume the responsibility of assisting and training teachers to work with children who have special problems. Schools suffering a lack of adequately trained teachers have a responsibility to inform college administrations of this need.

General Procedure

We propose this general procedure for school districts:

1. *Commitment:* This commitment should be expressed by the school administration and board of education. Discover and face the fact that many children are not succeeding in the present programs. Children's needs and abilities differ, therefore methods and materials in education must differ. This must go beyond three reading groups, three tracks and watered-down curriculum. Once again we stress the need to be child-oriented rather than curriculum-oriented.

2. *A coordinator:* He should be trained to develop and implement, preschool through twelfth grade, a multisensory approach to help teachers meet the needs of children. This coordinator will not be effective unless adminstrative commitment is expressed to all school personnel to assure a change at the core of the school structure to pave the way for this job.

3. *Appropriate inservice training:* Initial and on-going inservice training should utilize existing knowledge available such as that obtained from local universities and special education programs. It also is possible to seek information and individuals from all parts of the country who are now working in this field. Inservice training must be available for principals, classroom teachers (preschool through twelve), physical education teachers, reading specialists, speech correctionists, pupil personnel, school psychologists, school social workers and school nurses. All school personnel must work as a team for the benefit of the child, rather than working separately.

4. *Special classes:* Although most children can be handled within regular classes we realize for some this is not feasible. Therefore, small self-contained classrooms are necessary. Whenever possible the child contained in these classrooms should have the opportunity of participating in any regular classes he can cope with.

5. *Evaluation:* Each child experiencing problems in the school

should have a thorough educational and psychological evaluation by personnel knowledgeable in the area of learning problems.

6. *Records:* Adequate files and reevaluation of the child, his methods and materials is essential, to be kept and used in central office. The best records are useless unless teachers understand and have access to them.

7. *Resource materials:* Availability and easy access to new methods materials and audiovisual aids in a central resource center is necessary.

8. *Parent education:* Because of the newness and complexity of the remediation of learning problems it is to the advantage of parents and educators to have extensive parent orientation. This establishes proper understanding and communication between home and school.

9. *Literature:* Encourage administration and teachers to seek help through any means available: newsletters, journals, films, conferences, workshops, lectures, and general literature. In-depth training via graduate programs and summer workshops also will be of interest. It is the responsibility of the administration to keep teachers informed.

SUMMARY STATEMENT

With our educational structure as it is today isn't the above impossible? It could be and may be—but we think not. If there is any way to help children, then it must be done and that is why we have shared with you our feelings and suggestions that might be helpful in an otherwise impossible situation.

The children need your help, for they are here—now—to stay. We can either assume the responsibility of helping them while they are young or we can assume the more expensive task of maintaining them as unproductive members of society.

As we become a more complex society it is even more important that we fit ALL men to live and govern this society, not become victims of an unaware, uninformed and apathetic community.

RESOURCE LIST

1. ASSOCIATION FOR CHILDREN WITH LEARNING DIS-ABILITIES, NATIONAL OFFICE, 2200 Brownsville Rd., Pittsburgh, Pa. 15210
2. ASSOCIATION FOR CHILDREN WITH LEARNING DIS-

ABILITIES, NATIONAL NEWSLETTER, "Items of Interest" ACLD newsletter Manager, Mrs. Blackstone Thompson, 912 South 81st St., Birmingham, Ala. 35206 ($2.00 for two years).

3. CANADIAN ASSOCIATION FOR CHILDREN WITH LEARNING DISABILITIES NEWSLETTER, 88 Eglinton Avenue East, Suite 318, Toronto 12, Ontario.

4. CALIFORNIA ASSOCIATION FOR NEUROLOGICALLY HANDICAPPED CHILDREN NEWSLETTER, 11291 McNab St., Garden Grove, Calif. 92641.

Literature

Up-to-date literature (order blanks on request) is available: Canadian Association for Children with Learning Disabilities, and California Association for Neurologically Handicapped Children (addresses as above).

Films

An up-to-date list of films, tapes and recordings is available: Canadian Association for Children with Learning Disabilities (addresses as above $1.00).

Journals

1. COUNCIL FOR EXCEPTIONAL CHILDREN, NEA, DIVISION FOR CHILDREN WITH LEARNING DISABILITIES, 1201 Sixteenth St., N. W., Washington, D. C. 20036 (dues CEC $15.00, dues D-CLD $4.00).

2. JOURNAL OF LEARNING DISABILITIES, 5 North Wabash Ave., Chicago, Ill. 60602 (one year $8.00, two years $12.00, special teacher and student rate $5.00 yearly).

3. ACADEMIC THERAPY, a quarterly, 1543 Fifth Ave., San Rafael, Calif. 94901 (one year $4.00, two years $7.50).

INDEX